Democracy Vouchers and the Promise of Fairer Elections in Seattle

Democracy Vouchers and the Promise of Fairer Elections in Seattle

Jennifer A. Heerwig and
Brian J. McCabe

TEMPLE UNIVERSITY PRESS
Philadelphia / Rome / Tokyo

TEMPLE UNIVERSITY PRESS
Philadelphia, Pennsylvania 19122
tupress.temple.edu

Library of Congress Cataloging-in-Publication Data

Names: Heerwig, Jennifer A., author. | McCabe, Brian J., author.
Title: Democracy vouchers and the promise of fairer elections in Seattle /
Jennifer A. Heerwig and Brian J. McCabe.
Other titles: Political lessons from American cities.
Description: Philadelphia : Temple University Press, 2024. | Series:
Political lessons from American cities | Includes bibliographical
references and index. | Summary: "Draws lessons from Seattle's
experience with its Democracy Voucher Program, an innovative public
campaign financing system designed to change how local elections are
funded"— Provided by publisher.
Identifiers: LCCN 2024014837 (print) | LCCN 2024014838 (ebook) | ISBN
9781439926253 (cloth) | ISBN 9781439926260 (paperback) | ISBN
9781439926277 (pdf)
Subjects: LCSH: Campaign funds—Washington (State)—Seattle. | Political
campaigns—Washington (State)—Seattle. | Seattle (Wash.)—Politics and
government.
Classification: LCC JK1991.5.W37 H44 2024 (print) | LCC JK1991.5.W37
(ebook) | DDC 324.7/809797772—dc23/eng/20240418
LC record available at https://lccn.loc.gov/2024014837
LC ebook record available at https://lccn.loc.gov/2024014838

To the RS

Contents

Acknowledgments

In 2017, the citizens of Seattle embarked on an unchartered path to transform the experience of local democracy. As their story unfolded, we had the good fortune of being on the sidelines each election cycle. Researching and writing this book has been one of the most rewarding experiences of our professional careers. We hope that the insights will prove valuable to other policymakers and advocates working to build more inclusive, fairer democratic systems.

Along the way, we encountered an extraordinary group of people who have brought the Democracy Voucher program to life. We owe our largest debt of gratitude to Wayne Barnett and René LeBeau at the Seattle Ethics and Elections Commission. Since we first met Wayne and René on our inaugural research trip, they have answered our endless questions, shared pristine data, and provided feedback on earlier drafts of this work. They are true models of public servants in their stewardship of Seattle's Democracy Voucher program. We are deeply grateful for their serious, sustained engagement with our project. Others at the Seattle Ethics and Elections Commission were invaluable as well. Polly Grow promptly fulfilled all our data requests. Annie Tran connected us with community groups around Seattle to learn about their work on the ground. Chrissy Courtney responded to our numerous technical inquiries. There is little doubt that the successful implementation of the program is due to this dedicated team.

In Seattle, we are also deeply grateful to Alan Durning at the Sightline Institute for being a thoughtful interlocutor and sharing his invaluable local expertise. Many other local candidates, activists, and stakeholders took the time to share their experiences with us as well. Without their involvement, we would not have the intimate knowledge of the program that comes with being a local. Finally, the Sociology Department at the University of Washington proved to be the perfect home as we started the research for this book.

This project would not have been possible without the support of Estevan Muñoz-Howard, who advocated for our research in both significant and subtle ways. Spencer Olson, Nick Nyhart, and Tam Doan generously shared our research with stakeholders and connected us with community resources. The Piper Foundation generously funded our research, and our program officer, Tiffany Mendoza, provided ongoing support to our project.

This work builds on the incredible contributions of several key scholars, but none more than Larry Lessig. We are grateful to Larry Lessig for his mentorship and for providing helpful feedback on earlier drafts of this work. Our colleagues in the sociology departments at Stony Brook University and Georgetown University continue to champion our scholarship and value its real-world impact. From those departments, we owe special thanks to Kenan Dogan and Rafferty Thompson, who provided skillful research assistance along the way. Aaron Javsicas and Richard Dilworth at Temple University Press have significantly strengthened this work and admirably guided it through the publication process.

Last but not least, our families have tolerated us for many years, and for that, we are especially thankful. Amanda Heerwig steered us through the funding process and encouraged us to persevere when we had almost given up. Even when we had doubts, Wayne Cecero; Brenda Heerwig; Leslie Henriques; Bonnie and John McCabe; Alice, Ray, and Sebastian Riegert; and Jadson Souza always cheered us on. We also owe a special thanks to our friends, who believe that rigorous social science research matters beyond the academy. Finally, a special shout-out to Keith Riegert for offering his wit and wisdom at all stages of this project.

Democracy Vouchers
and the Promise of Fairer
Elections in Seattle

Introduction

Political Reform in a Progressive City

N estled between Puget Sound to the west and Lake Washington to the east, the city of Seattle looms large in the progressive imagination. Represented in Congress by Pramila Jayapal, the chair of the Congressional Progressive Caucus, the city boasts a liberal political reputation. More than half of Seattle residents identify as Democrats, placing the city among the most liberal cities in the country, alongside San Francisco, New York City, and Washington, DC.[1] Accounting for the presence of self-identified Independents, Democrats in Seattle outnumber Republicans by four to one.[2] In the 2020 presidential election, Joe Biden sailed to victory in Seattle with more than three-quarters of the vote.

Seattle's liberal reputation has been reinforced in recent years by a robust, college-educated workforce in the booming tech sector. The headquarters of Amazon and Starbucks are both in Seattle, and Microsoft is headquartered in nearby Redmond. Other tech companies, including Google and Meta, keep a sizable base of employees in the Seattle region. The tech sector has contributed to the city's explosive population growth in recent years. Only two decades ago, Seattle was home to 563,375 people; by 2022, the city had grown to 749,265 people—a remarkable 34 percent increase.[3] Owing largely to the competitive salaries for the college-educated workforce, the expanding tech sector has fueled income growth for many residents.[4] The median income in Seattle increased more than 40 percent in the last decade, climbing from $74,823 (inflation-adjusted 2021 dollars) for the typical household in 2010 to $110,781 in 2021.[5] Alongside these demographic changes, the city has undergone remarkable changes in the built environment. Whole neighborhoods, such as South Lake Union and the Denny Triangle, home to Amazon headquarters, have been renewed and redeveloped.[6]

And yet, like many large cities in the United States, Seattle is experiencing pressing social problems that highlight deep fissures within the city. The tech sector has not brought prosperity to all Seattleites. Many of the challenges of managing and governing an increasingly unequal city are visible every day on the streets of Seattle. Even as the average income in the city has climbed, Seattle continues to wrestle with significant inequality and poverty. In 2021, the richest households in Seattle made about twenty-two times more than the poorest households.[7] In that year, Seattle ranked twenty-ninth out of ninety large cities in income inequality, up five places from 2018.[8] Inequality in the city is also strongly racially patterned. While nationally the average Black household earns about 60 percent of the average white household, in Seattle the average Black household earns just 35 percent of the average white household.[9]

At the same time, Seattle has a sizable population living without the means to pay for basic necessities like housing and food. About 11 percent of the population lives below the federal poverty line.[10] Although African Americans comprise only about 6 percent of the total population in Seattle (and whites, by contrast, comprise about 60 percent), they are disproportionately represented among the city's poor.[11] Over 33 percent of the Black population lives below the poverty line, compared to only 9 percent of the white population.[12] The persistent challenge of homelessness, exacerbated by a runaway housing market, underscores the consequences of inequality in the city.[13]

The Political Landscape of Seattle

Seattle is governed by a mayor-council system with officials elected for four-year terms. Primary elections are conducted using a nonpartisan "top-two" system in which the top two candidates go on to compete in the general election. Until recently, members of the Seattle City Council were elected to nine at-large seats, rather than through districted council elections. In 2013, voters approved Charter Amendment 19 to transform the structure of the City Council.[14] Beginning the following year, the council was restructured into seven district seats and two at-large seats, each of which is elected in a separate contest. Notably, districted elections create an opportunity for voters to elect representatives from their communities, a reform designed to ensure that the members of the council more accurately reflect the demographics of the constituents they serve.[15] Following the passage of Charter

Amendment 19, at-large council seats are now contested in the same election year as the mayoralty (e.g., 2017, 2021), and all seven districted seats are contested in the subsequent off-year election (e.g., 2019, 2023).

The city has a strong history of political activism and a citizenry that is unusually engaged in local politics. Despite this heightened level of political engagement, participation in local elections during off-year elections remains well below participation in statewide and federal elections. In 2020, 86 percent of King County residents cast a ballot in the presidential election.[16] The following year, when the top race on the ballot was the mayoral election, electoral participation fell dramatically. Only 55 percent of registered voters cast their ballot in this local race.[17] Even so, this level of voter participation in local elections dwarfs that in many other major cities with off-year local elections, such as New York City.[18]

Reflecting entrenched patterns of inequality within the city, resident engagement across Seattle neighborhoods remains uneven. In 2019, when the city held elections for the districted City Council races, participation varied from neighborhood to neighborhood. In District 6, which includes the northern neighborhoods of Ballard, Fremont, and Green Lake, 59.37 percent of eligible voters cast their ballots; by contrast, in District 2, which includes the southern neighborhoods of Columbia City, Georgetown, and the Central District, only 47.82 percent of eligible voters cast their ballots.[19] These patterns of uneven political participation reflect many neighborhood-level inequalities within Seattle, including differences in neighborhood incomes. While these gaps underscore unequal access to resources, time, and the ability to participate in the political process, they also reinforce political inequalities by ensuring that the voices of some residents are heard persistently in the political process, often to the exclusion of others.[20] In short, geographically patterned socioeconomic inequalities in the city are reflected in patterns of political inequality.

These socioeconomic inequalities manifest in other aspects of the political process, including contributions to political campaigns. Historically, local campaigns were funded by contributions from a small set of wealthy donors from within the city (as well as a donor pool living outside Seattle). Especially in mayoral elections, candidates relied on dollars from large donors, rather than grassroots contributors, to fund their campaigns.[21] Donors to local candidates disproportionately lived in a handful of wealthy neighborhoods, ultimately ensuring that the demands of those residents were represented in the political dialogue. In 2013, candidates for local office collected 25 percent of their money from donors in just 10 percent of Seattle neighborhoods.[22]

Even as Seattle wrestles with patterns of political inequality, the city has maintained a reputation for its left-of-center politics. In 2013, voters elected Kshama Sawant, a member of the Socialist Alternative party, to the City Council. With the election of Sawant, Seattle became the only American city in decades to have an elected representative from a socialist party.[23] But even before the arrival of Sawant on the political scene, Seattle had a long history of organized political protest. In the so-called Battle of Seattle in 1999, the meeting of the World Trade Organization (WTO) in Seattle drew tens of thousands of protestors concerned about the environmental impacts of globalization and its effects on everyday workers. More recently, the city gained notoriety for the Capitol Hill Organized Protest (CHOP), an organic political protest in the Capitol Hill neighborhood centered largely on progressive policy ideas, such as defunding the police and decarceration.[24] With a sustained history of progressive engagement in an increasingly unequal city, Seattle remains a place of deep contradictions. It maintains its liberal reputation, bolstered by the historic election of a socialist candidate to the City Council while continuing to wrestle with deepening patterns of social and economic inequality.[25]

Progressive Politics and Political Innovation in the Pacific Northwest

While Seattle faces challenges that are typical of American cities in an era of growing inequality, the city is unique in one important regard. Building on its reputation as a bastion of progressive politics, Seattle is at the forefront of policy innovation and reform to address these difficult challenges. Across a handful of policy arenas, Seattle is leading the way. In fact, political leaders from across the country point to Seattle as an example in setting the national agenda for policy change.[26] The structure of local governance in Seattle allows citizen-led ballot initiatives and referenda on legislation passed by the council.[27] Ballot initiatives empower citizens to propose legislation for direct review by voters, while referenda enable citizens to voice their approval (or disapproval) of legislation passed by the council. Both vehicles ensure that citizens' voices are heard directly in the political process. These forms of direct democracy deepen citizen engagement in addressing policy concerns.[28]

Among its most significant progressive policy reforms, Seattle led the way in the fight for a fair minimum wage to address pay inequalities in the workforce.[29] In 2015, Seattle became the first city to embrace a $15 per hour minimum wage. Political leaders in Seattle mandated other protections for workers in the city as well. The City Council passed the Gig Worker Paid

Sick and Safe Time Ordinance to mandate sick leave for workers in the gig economy.[30] In 2018, Seattle became the first American city to pass a Domestic Workers Bill of Rights.[31] As Seattle grapples with a growing crisis of housing affordability, the city has also been at the forefront of progressive policies to ease the housing burden and combat discrimination in the rental market. The city's "first-in-time" rule requires landlords to rent their units on first-come, first-served basis.[32] The law is intended to combat discrimination in the provision of housing by mandating that landlords accept the first qualified applicant to their unit. Across a range of policy areas, city leaders in Seattle have positioned the city as a hub for innovative, progressive policy experimentation. Building on this long-standing commitment, Seattle has emerged as a national leader in campaign finance reform.

Planting the Seeds of a Campaign Finance Reform Movement

In 2015, voters in Seattle approved a ballot initiative, the Honest Elections Seattle (HES) Initiative (I-122), to transform the financing of local elections. While I-122 included a handful of other reforms, the most significant change, and the subject of this book, was the creation of the nation's first democracy voucher program.[33] With the support of nearly two-thirds of Seattle voters, Seattle would lead the way into a new era of campaign finance.

Each election cycle, the city would provide Seattle voters with four $25 democracy vouchers that they could assign to the local candidate of their choice. Voters would be able to assign their vouchers to candidates running for City Council, mayor, or city attorney. By providing resources to *every* Seattle resident to participate in financing the election, the Democracy Voucher program would create a new, participation-centered model of public financing for local elections—a model that had never been tested before in American politics. If successful, this policy innovation would improve representation, deepen democracy, and ensure fairer elections in cities nationwide.

At the same time, the passage of the Democracy Voucher program and its implementation raised pressing questions about translating this far-reaching reform into practice. One set of questions concerned the actual design and implementation of the innovative program. How would the Seattle Ethics and Elections Commission implement the program? What types of administrative and bureaucratic obstacles would be encountered along the way? Other questions centered on the response of voters and candidates to the program. Would the Democracy Voucher program solve the problems of unequal representation in local politics by bringing new donors into the political system? Would the program attract nontraditional candidates to run for elective office? Would those changes have long-term policy impacts on the progressive city? Leveraging data from three election cycles, this book sets out to answer those questions.

In the next chapter, we trace the origins of this innovative campaign finance idea. To understand *how* the initiative got to the ballot in Seattle, we start with a history of where the idea of "democracy dollars" originated. The proposal for a system of "democracy dollars" provided directly to residents to fund political campaigns emerged from broader efforts to reduce the influence of wealthy donors in American elections. Unlike other public campaign finance reforms, the program is uniquely centered on increasing participation and ameliorating the longstanding representational inequalities of private donations. While scholars and activists tend to focus on these issues in federal elections, it is perhaps fitting that the first to implement this program was a local government.[34] Money plays a distinct role in municipal elections—a role rarely captured in the focus on federal fundraising. By describing how the idea for a voucher program landed on the ballot in Seattle, we emphasize the unique problems of local democracy and municipal politics that the voucher system set out to solve.

In Chapter 2, we offer an empirical evaluation of the impact of the Democracy Voucher program. Through the framework of participation, renewal, and representation, we answer critical questions about whether the program has fulfilled the goals set out by the reformers and activists. We analyze local administrative records from the Seattle Ethics and Elections Commission and report on interviews with local candidates to better understand *how* the program is transforming local elections. Overall, the Democracy Voucher program has drawn many thousands more Seattleites into the campaign finance system. These voucher users represent a new cohort of participants, renewing the pool of donors with each local election. Perhaps most critically, these voucher users are more representative of voters as a whole than are cash donors. The program has also shown strong gains in its impact on local candidates. Electoral competition in Seattle's local elections has skyrocketed. Seattle's local elections now attract a much wider and more diverse field of candidates for local office. But even with these successes, there is more work to do. People of color and less affluent and younger residents continue to participate at lower rates than other groups. The Democracy Voucher program is an important step forward, but it is not a panacea for all that ails local democracy.

In Chapter 3, we examine challenges to the legitimacy and longevity of the Democracy Voucher program and, more broadly, to the system of publicly funded vouchers. On one hand, we point to the inherent tradeoffs of designing and implementing this innovative program. We identify key challenges in program design, candidate participation strategies, and citizens' engagement from the experience in Seattle. On the other hand, we consider external threats to the program from litigation over the constitutionality of a voucher program and the rise of independent expenditures. Following the launch of the Democracy Voucher program, independent expenditures on behalf of candidates flooded local elections, raising anew concerns about undue political influence. Although the program was designed to limit the reliance of individual candidates on big donors, the rise of independent expenditures represents an existential threat to the program. By identifying both internal and external threats to the program, we identify key issues related to the design, implementation, and legitimacy of future programs.

In the Conclusion, we identify a pathway forward for progressive campaign finance reforms like the Democracy Voucher program. In many ways, Seattle is an ideal place to experiment with this innovation. The rich history of progressive politics and citizen-led initiatives created opportunities for political reform in the city. The city's history with campaign finance reforms created an opening for advocates to advance the Democracy Voucher program. Although activists and reformers have pushed to replicate the program elsewhere, other cities have been slow to build on Seattle's success. As we conclude the book, we identify opportunities for other cities to advance campaign finance reforms modeled on the experience of Seattle and the obstacles that will likely stand in their way.

Cash Is King

The Challenges of Money in American Politics

Most research on the campaign finance system and the influence of money in politics comes from analyses of federal, rather than local, elections. This focus on federal elections is well placed. Federal elections are incredibly costly, have grown more so over time, and have historically attracted donations from only a very small share of the electorate. They are also far more visible to average Americans, and they often revolve around issues with deep social and moral resonance.

Nevertheless, local elections are critically important to the everyday experiences of voters. Local governments make decisions about land-use planning, property taxation, public spaces, and public safety. Collectively, these decisions fundamentally shape the character of a community and the quality of the surrounding built environment. Given the relatively smaller arena of city politics, money plays a unique—and often overlooked—role in local elections. Although the typical local election is less expensive than the typical federal election, the true cost of local elections is significantly greater when viewed in the context of the low voter turnout in these contests. Concerns that emanate from money in federal elections are just as—if not more—pertinent to local elections.

After orienting the reader to the core debates about the effects of money on American politics, this chapter reviews the current regulatory context that sets the broad limits and possibilities for local reform. We outline why public campaign financing has emerged as one of the only remaining viable tools for reformers to address the issue of money in politics. After describing the two most common types of public financing programs, grants-based programs and public matching programs, we trace the intellectual genesis of the "democracy dollars" idea in legal scholarship. We then examine how the idea took root in Seattle and the coalition of local activists and advocacy organizations that led to a successful ballot initiative in 2015. Together, this chapter seeks to introduce readers to the problem of money in local politics and describe the unique movement to launch an innovative public financing program in Seattle.

The Problem of Money in American Politics

In 2020, political spending in federal races collectively topped more than $14 billion, exceeding the annual GDPs of roughly fifty countries.[1] These spending totals grew astronomically over the preceding two decades. In 2000, the typical winning candidate for the U.S. House of Representatives spent about $1.40 million. The winning U.S. Senate candidate spent about $11.95 million. By 2018, these costs had grown by 70 percent for House candidates and 42 percent for Senate candidates to $2.40 million and $17.05 million, respectively (all figures are in 2022 dollars).[2] In short, there's a lot of money in American elections.

At the most basic level, candidates need campaign cash to run their campaigns and get their message out to voters. Candidates use their campaign war chests to produce online and offline media to target persuadable voters, hire political consultants to hone campaign strategies, pay campaign staff, and commission polling to gauge their electoral prospects.[3] This dependence on campaign cash has implications for candidate behavior and campaign strategy. For one thing, candidates report spending significant amounts of time on fundraising.[4] Fundraising has become both a necessity and an institutionalized responsibility for candidates of both political parties. The ever-rising cost of running for office creates institutional and competitive pressures to prioritize fundraising at the expense of other activities, including interacting with voters and constituents. The high fundraising threshold for candidate viability—especially in primary elections—may also discourage potential candidates without deep pockets or networks of wealthy friends and colleagues from seeking elective office in the first place.[5] This dependence on fundraising widens the gap between the people who run for office and the people they represent.

Most of the money in the federal system comes from individual donors. For House candidates, individual donors supplied about 70 percent of total candidate campaign funds in 2020. This percentage climbs to nearly 90 percent for Senate candidates.[6] Individual donors are now, more than ever, the lifeblood of the federal campaign finance system. As we note later on, candidates are far more reliant on large individual donors (defined as those who give more than $200) than small donors.[7] Despite media attention to the increase in small donors, the average House candidate receives a paltry 10 percent of their funds from small donors and over 50 percent from larger donors (those giving more than $200).[8] Candidates who rely exclusively on small donations are still few and far between, even in the age of Internet fundraising.

The focus on fundraising deepens inequalities within our political system in another way. Only a tiny percentage of Americans contribute money to political candidates, raising the prospect that our system of campaign finance exacerbates inequalities of political voice.[9] In 2018, about 0.47 percent of the American population gave $200 or more to federal political committees, but donations of this size constituted about 71 percent of total funds.[10] Disparities in participation appear throughout the political system, including for voting, volunteering, and even talking about American politics, but the inequalities in contributing to campaigns are particularly stark.[11]

These steep inequalities in the campaign finance system are compounded by the characteristics of individuals in the donor pool. Donors contributing over $200 are wealthier and better educated than the typical American.[12] They are much more likely to be white and to be men. People of color comprise 9 percent of the federal donor pool but 29 percent of eligible voters, raising issues of racial equity and justice. Donors in America are even whiter than Congress itself.[13] In short, on a host of sociodemographic dimensions, donors in federal elections are descriptively unrepresentative of the electorate, undermining the principle of equal voice in American elections.

Evidence from both qualitative and quantitative studies points to the ways that money facilitates access to representatives—ways that being a mere voter does not. In one study of corporate giving in national elections, a long-time donor remarked to the interviewer that without regular campaign contributions, he "wouldn't have the access" to his elected representatives.[14] This qualitative evidence is bolstered by a recent field experiment that underlined the strong link between money and access. When randomized to a treatment group receiving an email from a political donor, members of the House of Representatives were five times more likely to offer a meeting with senior staff than to a nondonating constituent.[15]

Finally, our system of privately funded elections is likely one reason why average Americans have little or no influence over policy outcomes, at least at the national level. Evidence for so-called vote-buying has been mixed, but there is a strong correlation between the preferences of the affluent and business groups with policy outcomes across a range of issue areas.[16] Money is likely a central way that this distortion is produced.[17]

Money in Municipal Elections

The influence of money in American politics undermines the principle of political equality and gives donors unequal access to policymakers. While these concerns are evident in federal elections, they may be even more significant in races for local office where a confluence of factors heightens the salience of participation. Unlike members of Congress, who regularly represent 700,000 constituents, the typical city council member represents a much smaller constituency.[18] In Seattle, each of the seven districted City Council positions represents about 100,000 constituents. Depending on the population of a city and the size of the city council, district populations may be significantly smaller. This ensures easier access for constituents to interact with their locally elected representatives. In fact, much of the work being done by local representatives involves constituent services in the local arena.[19]

Municipal elections are also notorious for low levels of voter engagement.[20] Especially in cities that hold local elections in off-year cycles, voter turnout rates regularly fall below (already low) turnout rates for national office. In the off-year 2021 general election in Seattle, which included an open election for mayor, only 55 percent of registered voters cast a ballot. By contrast, 86 percent of King County residents voted in the 2020 general election.[21] These truncated levels of voter participation in local elections are common in American cities, especially when local elections are not held concurrently with elections for statewide or federal office.

Viewed through the lens of low participation, the millions of dollars spent in local races take on increased salience. While data cataloging contributions and expenditures in local races is harder to come by than for state and federal races, estimates for some of the largest cities in the United States provide evidence on the costs of funding municipal campaigns. In Figure 1.1, we compare the cost of open mayoral races in San Francisco, Los Angeles, Chicago, New York, and Washington, DC, to the cost of midterm House races in 2014 and 2018. For each city, we adjust total receipts in open mayoral races to reflect the number of registered voters in each jurisdiction. Since local elections are notorious for their low levels of turnout, we also calculate the raw cost per active voter in each election. In other words, how much did each vote cast "cost"?

When viewed this way, the true cost of local elections becomes clear. Although there is wide variation across city contexts, local elections consis-

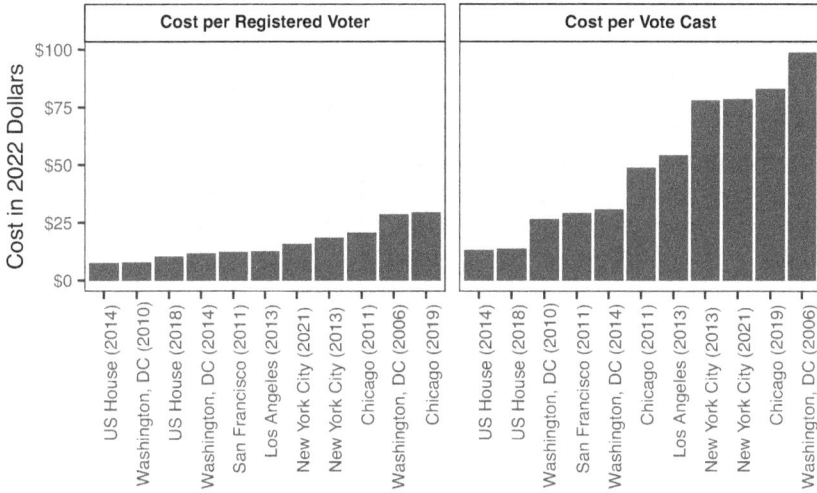

Figure 1.1: Cost of Open Mayoral Contests and Off-Year U.S. House Elections in 2022 Dollars

tently cost more per registered voter—and especially per vote cast—than U.S. House races. On average, elections for each city's open mayoral race cost about $18 per registered voter and $59 per vote cast. This compares to just $9 and $13, respectively, for the average House race. Admittedly, this comparison is far from perfect. It likely obscures variation across cities and states in the cost of different media markets as well as differences in population characteristics and political culture that affect campaigning. Yet, this back-of-the-envelope calculation allows us to provide a very rough estimate of the "cost" of elections across local contexts. It certainly suggests that concerns about money in American elections are just as—if not more—significant in local races.

Despite the cost of local elections, there is a more limited body of research on who finances municipal elections and how these patterns shape local governance. Drawing on a rich tradition in urban political economy, much of the existing research has focused on the business interests represented by fundraising coalitions of mayoral and city council candidates.[22] While this frame is important, it neglects other crucial aspects of representation that pervade local politics, such as deep and persistent inequalities based on race.[23] Recent evidence indicates local governments represent their white, wealthy residents to the exclusion of people of color and the less affluent.[24] These biases are reflected in policy outcomes on local issues such as housing development.[25] The high cost of local elections plays a critical role here as well. Money in local elections exacerbates inequalities of political voice and constitutes a high barrier to running for local office.

Solutions to the Problem of Political Money

Concerns about the representational disparities created by our system of private campaign financing are as old as the modern campaign itself. Recognizing the potential for undue influence over candidates and elected representatives, the U.S. Congress passed the first significant piece of campaign finance legislation in 1907 in response to corporate contributions in the 1904 presidential election. This section describes the broad legal framework that regulates money in American elections to contextualize the novelty and promise of the democracy voucher model.

Federal law regulates money in American elections in two primary ways: contribution limits and disclosure requirements. First, federal law limits the size of donations a private citizen can give to any one political candidate or political committee in a federal election. For instance, in the 2021–2022 election cycle, individuals could give up to $5,800 to a federal candidate in the primary and general elections combined.[26] Private citizens, however, can give to as many political candidates and committees as they wish.[27] Second, political donations exceeding $200 must be disclosed to the Federal Election Commission (FEC). These disclosure filings are then made available to the public for viewing and inspection.[28] State and local governments often enact their own contribution and disclosure requirements for elections in their jurisdictions.

Importantly, although the U.S. Supreme Court has struck down some forms of campaign finance regulation, it has upheld the constitutionality of public campaign financing programs. In a landmark case we discuss in Chapter 3, the court reasoned that public financing programs serve "to *facilitate* and *enlarge* public discussion and *participation* in the electoral process, goals vital to a self-governing people."[29] The case broadly affirmed the value of public campaign financing and created an opening for states and localities to design programs to meet these goals.[30] Today, more than three dozen states and municipalities have public financing programs—and more and more cities are adopting them each year.[31]

Public campaign financing programs provide candidates with public funds to run their campaigns. In exchange for public monies, participating candidates agree to adhere to a set of program rules. Generally, public campaign financing programs also package more stringent contribution limits and overall spending limits as a condition of a candidate's participation. Public campaign finance programs reduce candidates' dependence on big donors, freeing up candidate time to interact with voters and containing the costs of running for office.[32]

Types of Public Campaign Finance Programs

One set of programs, largely known as *Clean Elections* programs, provides full or partial public funding to candidates upon qualifying for the program.[33] These grants-based programs help relieve candidates of the challenges of fundraising. For instance, statewide candidates in Connecticut are eligible for a lump-sum grant to run for elective office after receiving small-dollar qualifying donations.[34] Many grants-based systems across the United States are now defunct or have fallen out of favor with policymakers. Municipalities such as Chapel Hill, NC, and Austin, TX, implemented grants-based programs, but the programs are no longer in use.[35] There are multiple reasons why these programs are declining. The size of the public grant to candidates must be continually revisited and updated to remain an attractive option for candidates. Skeptics have questioned funding for the programs during economic downturns when resources are scarce.[36] Most important, grants-based systems provide candidates with public campaign funds without directly incentivizing participation by citizens or encouraging candidates to interact with their future constituents.

The second set of programs provides public matching funds to candidates to amplify the contributions of qualified, small-dollar donors. Under these matching programs, candidates qualify to receive matching funds after demonstrating a base of political support and agreeing to contribution limits from individual donors. In turn, donations from individual donors are matched with public funds to magnify the contributions of these donors. Matching funds systems are currently the most widely used system of public campaign financing in the United States. At present, more than twenty states and municipalities have a matching funds program, including cities such as Los Angeles, New Haven, CT, and Washington, DC.[37]

New York City has one of the oldest matching funds programs in the country. The program was first implemented in 1989 and includes candidates running for mayor, public advocate, comptroller, borough president, and city council. Under the rules of the program, candidates demonstrate viability by first collecting a minimum number of contributions. For instance, mayoral candidates must collect a minimum of 1,000 contributions totaling at least $250,000 to be eligible for the program.[38] After this threshold has been met, each small-dollar donation a candidate receives is matched with public funds at a specified rate. In 2023, the matching rate stood at eight to one. For every $1 of a small-dollar contribution for that race, the candidate receives $8 in public funds.[39] For instance, a donation of $10 would generate a public match of $80 for a total of $90.

Matching funds aim to amplify the voices of small donors while less-ening candidates' dependence on large donors. In New York City, the matching funds program has produced gains in the number of small con-tributors and the diversity of neighborhoods funding local elections.[40] The neighborhood characteristics of small donors in New York City closely reflect the overall racial and economic diversity of the city, although the characteristics of individual donors participating in the program remain unknown.[41]

While matching funds systems ease the burdens of running for office, lessen candidate dependence on large contributions, and incentivize wider citizen participation in elections, they also reproduce some of the inequali-ties of the private financing of elections. Since matching funds systems supplement but do not replace private contributions, small-dollar donors may still be a relatively affluent slice of the engaged public. After all, even a donation of $10, $15, or $50 is out of reach for many American households (for example, those who live near the poverty line or rely on public assis-tance programs). Matching funds programs may amplify the voices of exist-ing donors while doing comparatively less to attract new donors into the campaign finance system.

Recognizing some of the shortcomings of existing public campaign fi-nance programs, reformers proposed a radically new approach: democracy dollars. By greatly expanding the supply of campaign cash, the democracy dollars idea sidesteps some of the criticisms of other more static public fi-nancing regimes.[42] Instead, the democracy dollars idea relies on an unre-stricted marketplace of donations to finance political candidates and facili-tates citizen engagement early in the election process.

Theorizing Democracy Dollars

The idea of a radically new type of public campaign financing system first germinated in legal scholarship on campaign finance reforms. Such pro-grams have variously been called "democracy vouchers," "patriot dollars," and "democracy dollars." While the proposals differed in detail, the broad outlines of the system remained the same. Unlike a grants-based system, democracy dollars would incentivize candidates to canvass and interact di-rectly with their constituents to collect campaign cash. Unlike a matching funds system, citizens would not need their own disposable income to par-ticipate in funding American elections. Democracy dollars would be avail-able to every citizen to spend on the candidates of their choice. With democ-racy dollars, candidates would rely on a diverse set of voters to fully fund their campaigns, rather than relying on a wealthy slice of the electorate.

The first systematic proposal for a democracy voucher program dates back more than thirty years.[43] Writing in the pages of the *American Prospect* in 1993, Yale law professor Bruce Ackerman envisioned a radically new type of campaign finance system.[44] In this initial statement, Ackerman imagined providing each American voter with a $10 Patriot credit card to make donations to federal political campaigns. Candidates participating in the program would forego cash donations completely and be solely dependent on "Patriot" donations. By becoming the sole coin of the realm, Ackerman argued that the "Patriot" program would "insulate campaign finance from the unmediated rule of money."[45] The "Patriot" program would extend the promise of political equality into the sphere of campaign finance, giving every American a voice in financing political candidates.

In 2002, Ackerman, together with fellow Yale law professor Ian Ayres, elaborated the details of their proposed democracy dollar idea in the book *Voting with Dollars*.[46] They argued that the campaign finance system in America was fundamentally broken. Reforms designed to simply regulate the amount of money in the political system or ensure more transparency in the financing of elections ultimately failed to get to the root of the problem of money in politics. Ackerman and Ayres argued that the existing approach to regulating money in politics—namely, setting limits on donations in much the way the Environmental Protection Agency (EPA) would regulate an environmental toxin—had failed.

Rather than regulating the system into compliance, they argued that political reformers needed a new approach guided by the principles of voting to fundamentally transform the way campaigns were funded.[47] Ackerman and Ayres offered a comprehensive alternative model of public financing that would *not* require the expenditure of private funds to earn a public match. Instead, the Patriot Dollars program would provide every voter with money to spend on the candidate of their choice. Ackerman and Ayres proposed a $50 voucher for federal elections. Writing about the idea in the *California Law Review*, University of Chicago legal scholar David Strauss later called the voucher idea "bracingly ingenious."[48] Indeed, the Patriot Dollars idea planted the seed that would later grow into a movement for political reform beginning in Seattle.

As they outlined the proposal for Patriot Dollars, Ackerman and Ayres argued that such a public financing system would avoid many of the pitfalls of the existing campaign finance system and the bureaucratic entanglements of "clean money" public campaign financing programs. Ackerman and Ayres suggested that providing every American voter with Patriot Dollars would create a "patriotic marketplace" for campaign funding. By decentralizing the public financing process, the Patriot Dollars system would allow voters a greater say in democratic deliberation, bringing them into the electoral process well before Election Day and empowering them to shape the electoral agenda. The sea of Patriot Dollars available to potential candidates would also encourage candidates to tap into collective sentiments and unmet political demands. Importantly, Ackerman and Ayres envisioned the Patriot Dollars system coupled with a "secret donation booth" for private donations. By anonymizing private political donations, the two-pronged approach to public campaign finance would reduce the motivation of big donors to buy access and prevent candidates from favoring their largest contributors.

Nearly a decade after the publication of *Voting with Dollars*, Harvard legal scholar Lawrence Lessig popularized the proposal in his 2011 book *Republic, Lost: How Money Corrupts Congress—and a Plan to Stop It* and in a widely read op-ed that appeared in the *New York Times*.[49] Building on Ackerman and Ayres, Lessig argued that the growing influence of money in politics is contributing to the erosion of American democracy. Importantly, Lessig urged his readers to reconsider their conception of the current private system of campaign cash. Private campaign cash pulls candidates and representatives away from the needs of their voting constituencies. The relentless search for campaign cash serves to distract candidates, distort the legislative agenda, and undermine trust in the legislative process.[50]

Lessig proposed a system of democracy vouchers modeled on the Patriot Dollars program. Each voter would receive $50 in vouchers to allocate to the congressional candidate of their choice. Voters would decide how to use their vouchers. They could allocate all $50 to a single candidate, or they could split their vouchers among multiple candidates. Lessig's plan included an alternative to the private donation booth: candidates participating in the program would simply agree to lower contribution limits from private donors. Individuals would be allowed to contribute up to $100 of their own money to a candidate, in addition to the voucher, but no more. For their part, candidates who agreed to participate in the voucher program would foreswear contributions from political action committees and political parties. As Lessig wrote, "The only external funds such a campaign would receive would be democracy vouchers plus, at most, one Ben Franklin per citizen."

Writing in *Republic, Lost*, Lessig also clearly articulates why this system of vouchers is superior to other forms of campaign finance reform. For one thing, the system does not require individual donors to front their own money in campaigns and elections. By providing everyone with an opportunity to participate in the campaign finance system, a democracy voucher proposal would level the playing field and broaden the opportunities for citizens to engage. Perhaps more important, candidates and elected officials would never be beholden to interest groups, as they are in the current campaign finance system. Under a program of citizen-financed democracy vouchers, there would be no wealthy donors to blame for the decisions of Congress. Moreover, since democracy vouchers would be financed from general tax funds—as Lessig writes, the first $50 of each payer's tax bill would be used to fund their own vouchers—there could be no claims that taxpayer money was going to fund political ideas that voters disagreed with.

In the years following the publication of *Republic, Lost*, Lessig brought his ideas to reformers across the country in a series of public lectures about the problem of money in politics. It is here that the intellectual history of democracy vouchers serendipitously intersects with the reform movement in Seattle. Just as Lessig traversed the country with his reform message, organizers in Seattle were regrouping after losing a referendum on a public matching program. Searching for an innovative alternative to a matching program, local organizers found just the answer in Lessig's work and the *democracy vouchers* idea.

The Movement to Reform Elections in Seattle

Before Seattle pioneered the Democracy Voucher program, the city had a long history of public financing in municipal elections.[51] In the late 1970s, Seattle was the first city to create a public financing program for municipal elections.[52] Under this inaugural program, participating candidates for city-wide office received a 1:1 match on contributions up to $50 in the 1979 and 1981 elections.[53] Beginning with this inaugural program, Box 1.1 provides a timeline of major milestones in the history of campaign finance in Seattle, ultimately leading to the passage of the Democracy Voucher program.

While the program proved to be an immediate success, a sunset provision in the legislation caused the program to lapse in 1982. The program was briefly reinstated for the 1987, 1989, and 1991 elections but came to an abrupt and final halt in 1992 with the passage of Initiative 134, which set forth state-wide contribution limits and disclosure requirements while also banning the use of public financing programs in state and local elections.[54] The law superseded the authority of the Seattle City Council to enact campaign finance legislation, thereby leading to the discontinuation of Seattle's matching funds program. While other cities, including New York City, had implemented matching programs by this point, Seattle reverted to private financing of local elections.

In 2008, the state partially amended the ban on public campaign financing passed in 1992. While the new law retained the prohibition on public funding of statewide elections, the legislature gave the green light to local programs that were approved by local voters and financed with local reve-

Box 1.1: Timeline of Events Leading to the Passage of Initiative 122 in Seattle

Date	Event
1978	Seattle becomes the first city in United States to enact public matching funds system for local elections
1979–1981	First city elections conducted with matching program
1982	Sunset provision in city ordinance ends matching funds program in Seattle
1984	Matching funds program reinstated by Seattle City Council
1987–1991	City elections conducted with matching program
1992	State initiative 134 bans public campaign financing programs in Washington
2008	Ban amended by WA legislature to allow for public campaign financing programs paid for by local funds
February 2013	Fair Elections Seattle launches campaign to bring publicly funded elections to Seattle
June 2013	Seattle City Council refers matching funds program to November ballot as Proposition #1
November 2013	Proposition #1 narrowly loses by 1,400 votes
January 2014	Fair Elections Seattle regroups after narrow loss and expands stakeholders
June 2014	Seattle City Council deadlocks on motion to refer matching funds proposition back to November ballot
Fall 2014	Expanded coalition decides to move forward with ballot initiative
Early 2015	Poll shows democracy vouchers idea more popular with voters, and coalition formally adopts plan
April 2015	Coalition launches public campaign for initiative (I-122) under banner of Honest Elections Seattle
November 2015	Honest Elections Seattle initiative wins decisively with 63% of voters in favor of I-122

nue sources.[55] Following this revision, the Seattle City Council proposed a matching funds program in 2013 with a 6:1 match of up to $50 in City Council races. To fund the matching program, Seattle residents would adopt an annual $2 million property tax levy. That November, the proposal was put to voters as Proposition #1.[56]

Behind the scenes, a loose coalition had begun organizing to support the passage of a matching funds program. Under the name Fair Elections Seattle, several local advocacy groups as well as a handful of unaffiliated activists worked together to pass the reform effort. The coalition, however, lacked buy-in from major progressive institutions in the area and ultimately raised only $109,000. Without significant resources to dedicate to the effort, the coalition was unable to effectively advertise the program to voters through mailers or a get-out-the-vote campaign before Election Day.[57]

In November 2013, voters narrowly rejected Proposition #1 to create a matching funds program. The proposition was rejected by a margin of only 1,400 votes—a much smaller margin than many organizers had anticipated, given the lack of resources the coalition was able to muster. As the organizer Estevan Muñoz-Howard put it, the group took this unexpectedly narrow loss as an opportunity to "fail forward." From the seeds of this failed initiative arose an opportunity to pursue a more innovative model for funding municipal elections.

The narrow defeat of Proposition #1 had another unanticipated consequence. It drew the attention of both local and national stakeholders who saw potential in Seattle for more dramatic democracy reforms. Throughout the early months of 2014, a newly emboldened coalition of civic organizations, including the Win|Win Network, Washington Community Action Network (CAN), and Fix Democracy First, met to strategize about a path forward for a public campaign finance program.[58] The discussion in these early months revolved around reviving the matching program effort through the Seattle City Council. The coalition of organizations hoped that, with additional local and national buy-in, the City Council would support another ballot referral for the 2014 midterm elections.

On June 30, 2014, the Seattle City Council deadlocked on a motion to refer the public campaign financing measure back to the ballot. At the time, there were already several tax measures slated for the November election, with two additional measures approved during the June 30 meeting. With other high-priority measures being put to voters, members of the council expressed concerns about reviving the public campaign financing measure so soon after its defeat in 2013.[59]

The City Council's decision to shelve the measure created a fortuitous political opportunity for the reform coalition.[60] Without the constraints of local city politics, the group was free to move beyond the framework of a matching funds program. With a ballot referral from the council off the table, the discussion about the future of the effort shifted to mounting a grassroots signature-gathering campaign for a voter-proposed ballot initiative. Over the next several months, the group's discussion also converged on a radically new model for financing elections in Seattle: democracy vouchers.

Honest Elections Seattle

Several factors account for the coalition's shifting momentum from pursuing a tried-and-true public campaign finance system to one that had never been implemented. For one, a local coalition partner, the Sightline Institute, briefed the group with possible scenarios for a voucher implementation in Seattle. Sightline's director and founder, Alan Durning, had studied the various proposals for democracy vouchers put forth by Lessig and others. Sightline's analyses helped the coalition envision how the program might function in their city, how much it might cost, and how participation in Seattle's elections could increase as a result.

The coalition subsequently commissioned a poll to test the popularity of the democracy vouchers proposal with voters. The poll showed that the idea of democracy vouchers was more popular than matching funds—a finding that spurred the group to formally vote on and adopt the democracy vouchers plan in early 2015. In the months that followed, the coalition continued to further test the viability of the democracy dollars idea with voters. In a focus group, Seattle voters expressed deep concerns about the influence of deep-pocketed developers in Seattle local elections and strongly supported the voucher proposal to restore equitable participation in city politics.[61]

Under the banner of Honest Elections Seattle (HES), the coalition launched a public campaign to gain voter approval for a package of electoral reforms that included the Democracy Voucher program.[62] The package, which was registered as Initiative 122 (I-122), proposed a number of other reforms, including a ban on contributions from corporations with large city contracts, an increase in penalties for election law violations, a requirement that signature gatherers disclose their funders, and a mandate for a "cooling off" period before former city officials could accept payment as local lobbyists.[63] While these policies were designed to increase transparency and accountability in local elections, it was the first-of-a-kind Democracy Voucher program that was at the heart of the Honest Elections Seattle proposal.

The proposal centered on providing four $25 democracy vouchers to eligible adults in Seattle to use in municipal elections. In its promotional materials, Honest Elections Seattle appealed to the innovative spirit of Seattle to help garner support for the novel program. The coalition touted Seattle's "legacy of pioneering community decisions" that had increased equity in the city.[64] The group cited a doubling of the average contribution size in Seattle between 2001 and 2011 as evidence of the growing clout of big money donors in local elections. In fact, in the 2013 election—the last election before the initiative for democratic reform appeared on the ballot in Seattle—about 65 percent of all money donated to local political candidates came from 1,683 people, or about 0.3 percent of Seattle residents.[65] The concentration of political money in Seattle closely mirrored national patterns and highlighted the need for reform.

With the implementation of the Democracy Voucher program, the coalition hoped to increase the number of contributors in municipal elections and "ensure everyone has the opportunity to have his or her voice heard, not just the wealthy and political elite."[66] Beyond direct participation in the campaign finance system, organizers for the Honest Elections Seattle campaign hoped to create a culture of participation in the city. By increasing participation in financing municipal elections, they hoped to generate sustained interest in local democracy and the electoral process. If they could engage everyday residents earlier in elections, these residents might be more likely to pay attention to issues, interact with political candidates, and cast their votes in notoriously low-turnout local elections. The program held the promise of addressing representational inequalities—the fact that the people who participate are descriptively unrepresentative of the people represented by elected officials—in the local political process.

By using public money to support political campaigns, the program could also "encourage a more diverse pool of candidates" to run for office.[67] If successful, it would attract the type of candidates who historically had been excluded from running for office because they lacked the wealthy donor networks required to finance a campaign. With nontraditional candidates seeking elective office, organizers expected the Democracy Voucher program to attract disengaged and disenchanted Seattle voters to re-engage with the political process. Across the board, organizers of the Democracy Voucher program endeavored to lessen candidates' reliance on high-dollar donors by limiting the role of private donations and providing every Seattle resident with money to contribute. Beyond its impact in Seattle, the Democracy Voucher program could also serve as the test case for local campaign finance reforms elsewhere.

By the time Election Day rolled around in 2015, the Honest Elections Seattle coalition had outraised and outspent its opponents—a move whose irony was not lost on those opposing the reform. The only organized political committee that opposed the initiative, No Election Vouchers, raised just $50,000.[68] It was vastly outspent—and out-organized—by the network of organizations and activists that supported the program. Voucher supporters raised nearly $1.4 million from just 174 donors to promote the program and mobilize voter support.[69] Nearly half of their money was raised from donors outside Seattle. Facebook cofounder Sean Eldridge, a New York resident who gave $200,000 in support of the reform, was among the largest donors to the Honest Elections campaign.[70]

Reflecting the strength of the Honest Elections Seattle coalition and the absence of significant organized opposition, support for I-122 was decisive.[71] On Election Day in 2015, about 63 percent of voters came out in support of the reforms. Acknowledging the leading role Seattle regularly played in progressive politics, Heather Weiner, a spokesperson for Honest Elections Seattle, compared the campaign finance victory to the minimum wage legislation Seattle had previously adopted. "Seattle leads the nation, first on $15 an hour and now on campaign finance reform. We look forward to seeing more cities and states implementing their own local solutions to the problem of big money in politics," she told the *Seattle Times*.[72] Following the lead of Seattle, officials in many other cities would be watching closely as the Democracy Voucher program got off the ground.

Conclusion

The Democracy Voucher program set out to solve the problem of money in local elections. As Ackerman and Ayres noted in *Voting with Dollars*, efforts to get money out of politics through contribution and spending limits had largely failed to stem the tide of campaign cash. The voucher model offered a different approach. It allowed for more cash in the political system to finance elections but ensured that those dollars came from a broad group of everyday Americans, rather than from a small pool of unrepresentative donors.

Although the lion's share of attention focuses on the role of money in federal elections, the pernicious effects of money in politics are felt strongly at the local level, where innovative, participation-centered public campaign financing offers a promising path forward. To date, small-donor matching programs have dominated the local landscape. Although matching funds incentivize candidates' reliance on small donors, they leave behind the many Americans who cannot afford even a small donation.[73]

In Seattle, the innovative Democracy Voucher program created a once-in-a-lifetime opportunity to ask whether an alternative model of funding campaigns can in fact radically shift modes of political participation. In principle, the voucher program allows everyone—regardless of income—to participate in the campaign finance system. By providing citizens with publicly funded vouchers to allocate to their favorite candidates, average city residents are brought into the electoral process well before Election Day. At the same time, the program should encourage more candidates to run for local office and to interact with their future constituents as they collect vouchers.[74]

Have these hopes been fulfilled? Has the democracy dollars model opened new democratic possibilities for both voters and candidates? Does the donor pool more accurately represent the electorate, and are the wide gaps in participation shrinking in response to the program? In short, has the untested program worked the way its architects intended? In the next chapter, we turn to an empirical evaluation of this first-in-the-nation public campaign financing experiment. Through the lens of participation, representation, and renewal, we examine how the program has changed the financing of local elections in Seattle, including whether the program has lived up to the expectations of national proponents and local organizers.

Honest Elections

Democracy Vouchers and the
Transformation of Seattle Politics

W hen the Honest Elections Seattle coalition coalesced around the novel idea of democracy vouchers, they envisioned a future where everyone would have their voices heard in local elections. By putting vouchers in the hands of all voters, reformers sought to increase engagement with local elections early in the campaign process. They hoped that the voucher program would enable Seattleites who were traditionally "priced out" of campaign finance to express support for their preferred candidates. As they sought to achieve these goals, reformers also hoped to create opportunities for candidates who might not ordinarily seek elective office given the daunting fundraising required to mount a successful campaign. By creating a broad base of financial support to attract a wider field of candidates, proponents expected the Democracy Voucher program to revitalize local democracy in Seattle. In doing so, the program could serve as a model for municipalities around the country. Without any precedent in the United States, the launch in Seattle would be an enormous test of the efficacy and opportunity for this novel campaign finance program.

In this chapter, we take a closer look at the impact of the Democracy Voucher program on local elections in Seattle. We focus on the first three election cycles, in 2017, 2019, and 2021, after the passage of the I-122 initiative. Our analyses center on three key themes impacting both voters and candidates: participation, renewal, and representation. To begin, we ask if the program is associated with increased *participation* in local elections. When reformers coalesced around the idea of democracy vouchers, they envisioned a program that would allow a much wider swath of Seattleites to engage in the local political process by putting money in the hands of average voters. While this infusion of cash would break the dependence of local candidates on a tiny core of affluent campaign donors, it would also give the average voter the resources to invest in the political process in a new and meaningful way.[1] In investigating *participation*, we ask whether more residents actually participated in financing local elections, and whether more citizens chose to seek elective office once the burdens of private fundraising were eased.

Second, we explore the ways in which the program has *renewed* the pool of participants in local elections. For residents in Seattle, renewal points to the emergence of a new generation of Seattleites investing in local politics, rather than continued participation of entrenched political donors. It also identifies the possibility of a new generation of candidates seeking local office as the advantages of incumbency wane. Third, we turn to the important question of *representation*. Contributors to American elections are notoriously "unrepresentative" of average Americans on every measurable dimension, including race, gender, age, and socioeconomic status.[2] If the Seattle program was a success, increased participation and renewal would lead to a more diverse, representative set of donors and local candidates.

The analysis that we lay out in this chapter points to the key success of Seattle's Democracy Voucher program, albeit with some noteworthy limitations. In each of the three election cycles that we analyze for this chapter, the Democracy Voucher program transformed participation in local elections. Compared to the elections prior to the program's implementation, more Seattle residents engaged in the campaign finance system in the era of democracy vouchers. In fact, Seattle now has one of the highest contributor rates in local elections for any city in America. This broader base of financial support has also enabled a wider field of candidates in local races. The program has also renewed the pool of donors in local elections, with new vouchers users constituting a core financial constituency during each cycle. This dynamism is also reflected among candidates with more competitive elections and fewer incumbents seeking re-election. Finally, the program has increased the representation of historically marginalized residents, including younger and less affluent voters, as well as people of color. The program is also associated with a shift in the demographics of candidates and elected officials. There are more women and people of color in elective office in Seattle, and the average age of candidates and elected officials has declined since the beginning of the program.

Building from the discussion in the previous chapters, these findings point to the ways the Democracy Voucher program is addressing some of the core challenges of local democracy. Municipalities around the country suffer from deep and systematic failures of representation. While this is true descriptively, as local candidates and elected officials are often quite dissimilar to their constituents along lines of race, class, age, and gender, it also impacts policy outcomes at the local level. The preferences of people of color and lower-income residents are routinely sidelined in local politics in favor of those of white and wealthy residents.[3] When participation is more equitable across groups, cities are more likely to have governing bodies that "look like them," and these bodies are more likely to implement policies that reflect the preferences and needs of these diverse constituencies.[4]

By increasing participation, generating renewal, and broadening representation, the Democracy Voucher program provides an important institutional pathway to improving the quality of local democracy. Of course, the program is not a panacea for all that ails city politics. Transformations to the campaign finance system need to happen alongside other reform efforts, such as easing the burdens of voter registration and improving turnout in local elections. But even after only three elections, the Democracy Voucher program has clearly increased citizen and candidate participation.

How the Democracy Voucher Program Works

After voters passed the Honest Elections initiative in 2015, the Seattle Ethics and Elections Commission (SEEC) implemented the Democracy Voucher program in the following election cycle. In 2017, residents could use their vouchers to support candidates in two at-large City Council races and the race for city attorney. In 2019, the program expanded to include the seven districted City Council races. In 2021, voters were permitted to use their vouchers in all municipal races, which included the contests for two at-large City Council seats, the city attorney, and the mayor. To better understand exactly *how* voters used their vouchers, we briefly describe core aspects of the program.

Candidates seeking elective office in Seattle have the option to use the Democracy Voucher program, but they are not required to participate. Once they opt into the program, they begin the qualifying process by signing a pledge to abide by all program rules. These rules include (1) adherence to lower contribution limits from individual donors than nonparticipating candidates for city council and city attorney races; (2) overall campaign spending limits for both the primary and general elections; and (3) participation in community-organized debates.[5] Table 2.1 provides an overview of the program's rules for participating candidates.

Contribution and spending limits vary by office. For instance, participating candidates running for an at-large City Council seat cannot accept

TABLE 2.1: PROGRAM RULES FOR PARTICIPATING CANDIDATES, 2023			
City Office	Signatures and Donations	Contribution Limit	Spending Limit[c]
Districted City Council	150[a]	$300	$93,750
At-Large City Council	400	$300	$187,500
City Attorney	400	$300	$187,500
Mayor	600	$550[b]	$400,000

Notes:
a. Includes 75 in district
b. Includes $50 in vouchers; contribution limit is the same for non-participating mayoral candidates
c. Candidates can reach the spending limits in Table 2.1 for both the primary and the general election

monetary contributions over $300; by contrast, nonparticipating candidates in an at-large City Council race can accept up to $600. Candidates also agree to limit their total election expenditures to a set amount in the primary and general elections. In 2021, candidates for at-large City Council races agreed to limit their total election expenditures to $375,000 (reflecting $187,500 in both the primary and general elections). These expenditure limits—as we discuss in Chapter 3—are updated every two years. Participating candidates can collect vouchers and cash donations so long as the combined total does not exceed the spending limit. By contrast, nonparticipating candidates do not face any spending limits in local elections, but they forego the available public money to finance their campaigns.

With these predetermined spending limitations for participating candidates, the implementation of the voucher program in Seattle diverged from the system theorized by legal scholars. Under Seattle's program rules, the *total amount any participating candidate can collect in democracy vouchers is determined by the expenditure limit for that election cycle, not by the number of available vouchers in the Seattle electorate.* For instance, a participating candidate running for mayor may collect up to $400,000 in democracy vouchers during the primary and general elections, for a total of $800,000 in democracy vouchers. Even if a candidate collects more than $800,000 in vouchers, the candidate cannot redeem them past the $800,000 limit. These spending limits have allowed the city to finance the program with a modest property tax levy of $3 million per year for ten years. At the same time, the limits have also led to practical difficulties, as we discuss in the next chapter.[6]

After pledging to abide by program rules, candidates begin a formal qualification process to demonstrate a minimum level of local, grassroots support before receiving public money.[7] Candidates qualify for the program by collecting both a specified number of contributions from small-dollar donors and signatures from Seattle residents (see Table 2.1). Qualifying contributions must be at least $10 but no more than the contribution limit for the office. However, the number of donors and signatures varies by office. For instance, candidates for at-large council seats must collect 400 qualifying contributions and signatures. After candidates meet these thresholds, they may begin redeeming vouchers from voters across the city.

During the period that candidates are qualifying for the program, the Seattle Ethics and Elections Commission (SEEC) mails every registered voter a packet of four $25 vouchers.[8] These vouchers are packaged in a bright blue envelope containing four perforated coupons to assign to local candidates. Voters can assign their vouchers to one or more candidates running for any eligible city office, including candidates running in City Council districts outside their own. Voters have several options to redeem their vouchers. They can do so by giving them directly to a candidate or campaign representative, mailing them back to the SEEC, dropping the vouchers in designated drop-off boxes around the city, or using the online portal that was launched in 2019.[9] As the program has matured, a growing share of residents have redeemed their vouchers through the online portal. In 2017, the first cycle of the program, most democracy vouchers were returned directly to the SEEC (78 percent) or given to candidate campaigns (20 percent). By 2021, a growing share of vouchers (21 percent) was assigned through the online portal.

The success of the Democracy Voucher program rested on the integration of historically marginalized groups into the new campaign finance system. To do so, the SEEC enlisted a variety of trusted community organizations to help voters understand the purpose of the program and navigate its logistics. Many of these organizations serve immigrant communities with high concentrations of nonnative English speakers, as well as student, LGBTQ, low-income, and unhoused populations. Since 2017, the SEEC has conducted hundreds of outreach events with a broad set of community organizations, including the Seattle Metropolitan Chamber of Commerce, the University of Washington Young Democrats, the API (Asian Pacific Islander) Coalition, and the LGBTQ Commission.[10] With the help of the SEEC, these organizations hosted formal presentations and distributed program information informally at community events to familiarize voters with the mechanics of voucher usage. Community organizations also facilitated distribution of voucher materials in many of the program's seventeen available languages, including Chinese, Thai, Vietnamese, Somali, and Russian. The network of community organizations the SEEC enlisted to inform voters— many of whom were unaware or even skeptical of the program in its early days—helped build a base of support for the Democracy Voucher program.[11]

Participation, Renewal, and Representation for Seattle Voters

Seattle's experiment with democracy vouchers aimed to increase voter participation in local elections and broaden and diversify the local donor pool. But has the program worked? After three election cycles, has the Democracy Voucher program reshaped participation, renewed the donor pool, and changed the representation of those financing local elections? In this section, we draw on a range of administrative records coupled with a proprietary voter file to understand the impact of the Democracy Voucher program on the financing of local elections.

Participation in the Democracy Voucher Program

In just three election cycles, the program has dramatically increased the number of Seattle residents who take part in financing local elections, giving them a voice in choosing the candidates who become contenders at the ballot box. In Figure 2.1, we plot the number of unique Seattle residents who gave a voucher, made a cash contribution, or did both in each election since 2013.[12] Notably, the number of cash-only contributors has remained relatively stable over time. By contrast, Figure 2.1 shows that participation in the voucher program has more than doubled in just three election cycles. In 2017, 20,727 Seattle residents participated in the program; by 2021, the num-

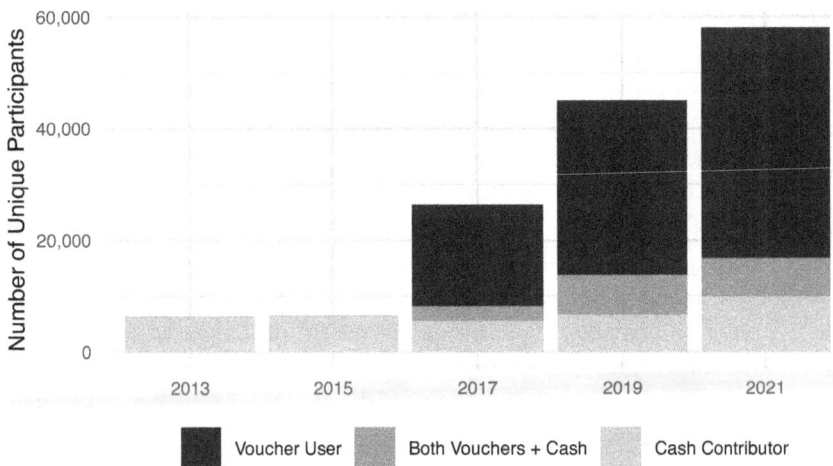

Figure 2.1: Number of Cash Donors and Democracy Voucher Users in Seattle Elections, 2013–2021

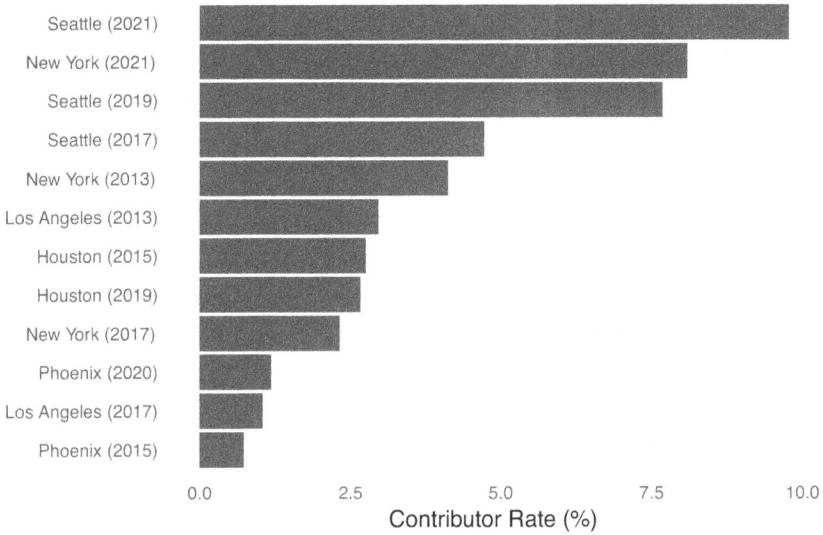

Figure 2.2: Contributor Rates as a Percentage of Registered Voters in Seattle, New York City, Los Angeles, Houston, and Phoenix (Local Election Years Only)

ber of voucher users rose to 48,071. The rise in participation is even more pronounced if we compare voucher usage to cash contributors before 2017. In 2013, about 6,000 Seattle residents contributed to a political candidate; by 2021, the number who contributed by giving cash or a voucher had risen to 58,000, a nearly 500 percent increase in participation.

With a growing number of Seattle residents participating in the campaign finance system, the Democracy Voucher program made Seattle a national leader in local participation. Figure 2.2 shows the contributor rate in Seattle relative to other large American cities. It identifies the number of contributors in local elections as a percentage of all registered voters in that election year. For Seattle, we count both unique voucher users and cash donors in our calculations. This figure likely overestimates participation in places like New York and Phoenix, where we assume each contribution represents one contributor. Still, Seattle's contributor rate is significantly higher than those of other major cities, such as Phoenix, Arizona, and Los Angeles. In 2021, nearly 10 percent of Seattle residents contributed to a local candidate, either by giving cash or redeeming a democracy voucher. Only in New York City in 2021, where nearly 8 percent of residents participated, was the contributor rate even close to Seattle's 10 percent. With the opportunity to contribute through vouchers or with cash, the contributor rate in Seattle has leapfrogged other American cities, underscoring the impact of the program in terms of integrating everyday residents into the political process.

Importantly, we also have good evidence that these impressive gains in Seattle were the direct effect of the Democracy Voucher program. In a study comparing local election funding in cities in Washington and California, Seattle stands out for what was termed the "enormous" growth in its donor base.[13] Compared to these other cities, the program in Seattle has significantly increased the number of small donors and the amount of funds from these donors. The rigorous statistical comparisons used in this study provide convincing evidence that the participation gains we see in Seattle are, indeed, the result of the Democracy Voucher program and not some other factor common across cities.[14] In plain terms, the program caused an explosion in participation in Seattle.

Renewing the Donor Pool

These dramatic increases in participation have been driven by an influx of first-time political donors. To complement our analysis of participation, we explore how the program has renewed participation in local campaign finance by recruiting new voters to "invest" in their local candidates. These first-time political donors point to an important shift in the campaign finance system in Seattle. Historically, repeat donors—those who give regularly across elections—have been a disproportionately influential constituency in American elections. Not only do these persistent donors give more money during each cycle, but they are also far more likely to report that they have regular contact with their representatives.[15] In this way, frequent donations become the currency of a lasting social relationship between the affluent and elected representatives.[16]

By contrast, the Democracy Voucher program has introduced a new dynamism into the financing of local elections in Seattle. To explore this aspect of the program, we utilize a panel of cash donors in Seattle who made donations in 2013 and 2015—the two elections prior to the implementation of the Democracy Voucher program.[17] Focusing on this group of cash donors, we can observe how their behavior changed as vouchers became available in 2017. One possibility is that established cash donors simply substituted vouchers for cash donations. Instead of using their own money, they used the money provided by the Democracy Voucher program. This scenario would suggest that the program has enabled the same core group of Seattleites to fund local elections but by using public monies.

In Figure 2.3, we look at how these established cash donors behaved in the first three cycles of the Democracy Voucher program. Overall, this analysis suggests that vouchers have supplemented, rather than replaced, cash donations for the Seattle "donor class." The plurality of established donors did not make another cash contribution or use a voucher after 2015. The second most common pattern was to supplement cash donations with de-

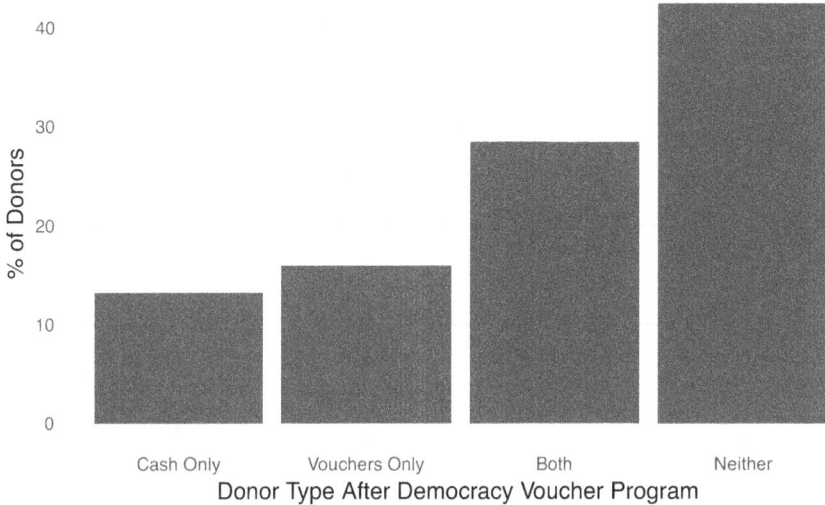

Figure 2.3: Giving Patterns of Established Cash Donors after Program Implementation

mocracy vouchers—around 30 percent of established donors continued to give cash *and* use their democracy vouchers. About equal percentages of established donors substituted their cash donations for vouchers as continued to give only cash donations.

As we illustrated in Figure 2.1, the voucher program greatly increased the number of participants in the local campaign finance system. Given that only a minority of established donors simply substituted their cash donations for vouchers, the program also effectively renewed participation in local campaign funding by encouraging a new wave of participants. At the same time, the large majority of voucher users redeemed vouchers in only one cycle between 2017 and 2021.[18] This suggests that the program has so far not produced a core of repeat voucher users who always participate in the program. One consequence of the program, then, was to dramatically decrease the concentration of repeat or "established" donors in local elections. Among the thousands of vouchers users and small cash contributors in each local election cycle, most are engaging in this form of participation for the first time, renewing the financing of local elections.

Increasing Representation in Local Politics

Along with these dramatic increases in participation, vouchers users are also more broadly representative of voters than are cash donors. To be sure, participation in the program is far from equal across sociodemographic groups. White, older, and more affluent Seattleites are more likely to use their vouchers than people of color and younger and lower-income citizens. Still, these remaining disparities in program participation are much smaller than the gaps in participation we observe in making a cash donation.

To examine participation across groups, we bring together data from the voucher program with a voter file containing sociodemographic variables.[19] In the panels in Figure 2.4, we plot program participation by three salient sociodemographic variables—race, age, and income. These three measures are strong predictors of political participation generally, including voting in elections, making a campaign donation, or volunteering for a campaign.[20] Race and income are also central axes of social and political inequality in the United States.[21] In Panel A, we compare the participation rate of non-Hispanic white voters to participation among people of color. For simplicity of presentation, we include Black, Hispanic, and Asian Seattleites in our "people of color" category and non-Hispanic whites in our "white" group. We replicate these findings in Panel B for participation by age category. Here, we compare participation among younger voters (those aged 18–44) to participation among older voters (aged 45+). Panel C examines participation for voters in lower-income ($0–$99,999 per year) households to voters in higher-income ($100,000+ per year) households.[22]

Taken together, the panels in Figure 2.4 illustrate three key patterns in participation across sociodemographic groups. First, all sociodemographic groups—young and old, rich and poor—have witnessed sizable gains in voucher usage since 2017. For instance, less than 3 percent of people of color redeemed vouchers during the program's first cycle, but that number climbed to over 6 percent by 2021. Panel B shows that 18- to 29-year-olds—who typically have the lowest voter turnout rates—also had the lowest program participation rate of any age group in 2017 at just 3 percent.[23] By 2021, participation among these younger voters had grown to 7.5 percent. Just under 5 percent of lower-income voters participated in the program in 2017 compared to nearly 9 percent in 2021 (Panel C).

Second, despite gains by historically marginalized groups, disparities remain in voucher usage within sociodemographic groups. This pattern persists across all three of our comparisons. Although younger residents made gains between 2017 and 2021, they remain significantly less likely to participate than older residents. These enduring gaps point to the persistent difficulty of broadening engagement in communities that have been traditionally overlooked in local politics. Participation in the voucher program has consistently been higher among white, older, and higher-income Seattleites than among people of color and younger and lower-income voters.

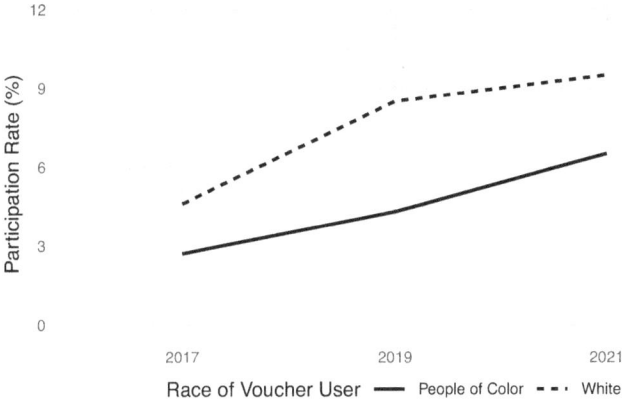

Figure 2.4a: Participation Rates by Race

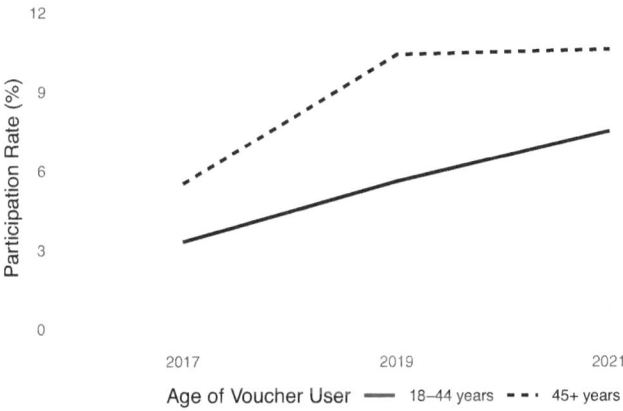

Figures 2.4b: Participation Rates by Age

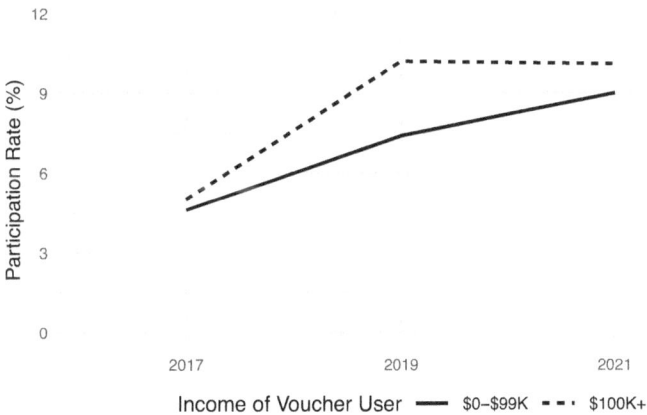

Figure 2.4c: Participation Rates by Income

Figure 2.4: Democracy Voucher Program Participation Rates, 2017–2021

Third, the observed gaps in voucher usage have varied by year—a finding that likely points to the idiosyncratic dynamics of each election and the differing slate of offices and candidates featured in each cycle. The most pronounced sociodemographic gaps appear in 2019, when Seattle's seven districted council seats were up for election. Although it is too soon to tell definitively, the relatively lower spending limits for those offices combined with the lower stakes of the districted elections could have exacerbated disparities in participation. In the 2021 election, which was the first to include the competitive and high-visibility mayoral contest, participation equalized significantly relative to the 2019 elections. Program participation among people of color and younger and less affluent voters climbed in 2021, ultimately narrowing the gap in participation substantially. In fact, the 2021 elections were a milestone for the representation of people of color and younger voters in funding local races. As the Seattle program matures, the extent to which program participation varies with office and candidate characteristics will become clearer.

Another metric to judge the efficacy of the program is to compare participation in the Democracy Voucher program to other forms of participation in the local arena. If the program broadens representation, we might expect democracy voucher users to more closely resemble voters (the most common form of political participation) than cash donors (an activity undertaken only by a relatively wealthy slice of the population). To the extent that those who fund local elections begin to look more like everyday voters rather than the pool of wealthy, older, and white cash donors that typically finance elections, then the voucher program reduces representational inequality. As a yardstick, we compare the democracy voucher pool to active voters and cash donors in local elections.[24]

To do so, we plot the representation ratio for three distinct forms of participation—voting in local elections, making a cash contribution, and using a democracy voucher—for people of color, younger people, and lower-income citizens. The representation ratio expresses the degree to which each group is under- or over-represented in a particular form of participation, compared to white, older, and higher-income citizens. Values less than 100 indicate that a group was under-represented, 100 indicates parity, and values greater than 100 indicate overrepresentation. If, for instance, 50 percent of people of color vote in local elections and 50 percent of white voters vote in local elections, the representation ratio for voting would be 100, indicating that the groups were equally likely to turn out at the polls. If, instead, 40 percent of people of color vote while 50 percent of white voters turn out, the representation ratio would be 80 for people of color indicating that their turnout rate was 80 percent of that of white voters. When the ratio dips below 100, as it does in Figures 2.5a–c, people of color are underrepresented in their participation; were it to climb above 100, it would suggest that they are overrepresented.

If the Democracy Voucher program is moving election funding in a more egalitarian direction, we should see the representation ratio for democracy voucher users come close to the representation ratio for voting. Again, voting is the most common—and most equal—act of political participation for Americans.[25] We also compare a group's representation among cash donors to its representation among democracy voucher users. If the program is working as intended, we should also find that democracy voucher users are more representative than cash donors. In sum, the representation ratio for voucher users should be closer to active voters than are cash donors.

The panels of Figure 2.5 show that the Democracy Voucher program has reduced racial, age, and income disparities in local elections. Figure 2.5a examines representation for people of color compared to white voters. From 2013 through 2021, there has been virtually no change in the representation ratio of voters of color in local elections. In other words, people of color are consistently underrepresented in the local electorate, with a representation ratio of about 60 across years. Figure 2.5a also shows that people of color are the most severely underrepresented among cash donors with a representation ratio ranging from 40 to 56. People of color have, however, been consistently better represented among democracy voucher users than among cash donors. Interestingly, we see representational inequalities widen in 2019—during the districted council elections—and narrow considerably in 2021. In the 2021 elections, people of color were better represented among democracy voucher users than among voters in local elections. In a measure of the program's success, the representation ratio for voucher users exceeded the ratio for voting among people of color.

Figure 2.5b shows that representation of younger Seattleites has increased markedly among democracy voucher users. In the pre-voucher period, the representation ratio was near 60 for voting in local elections and just 35 for cash contributions. Similar to the patterns by race, younger residents were far more underrepresented among cash donors than among voters. Compared to these stark age inequalities, representation of the youngest Seattle residents increased rapidly among voucher users in 2017 (although it fell noticeably in 2019 during the districted city council elections). Remarkably, the figure shows that—by the end of the series—the youngest Seattleites were better represented among Democracy Voucher users than among active voters, underscoring the potential of the program to energize participation in local politics.

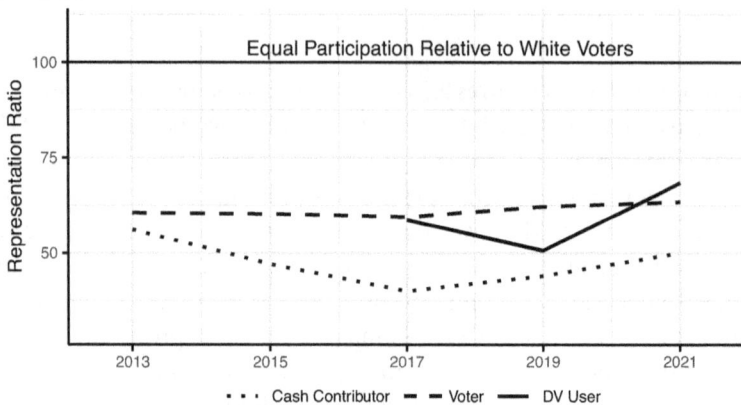

Figure 2.5a: Representation Ratios by Race

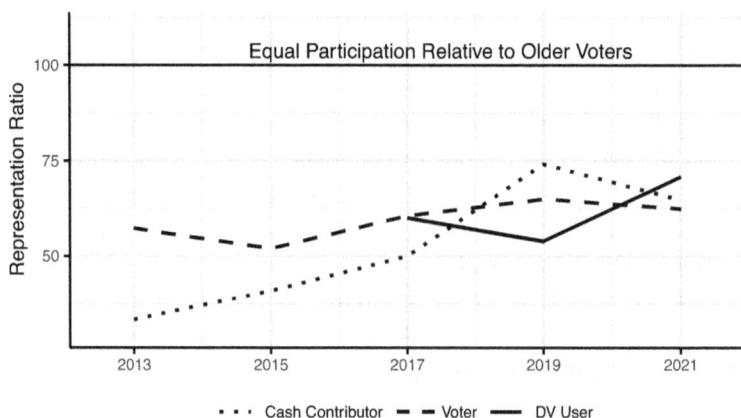

Figure 2.5b: Representation Ratios by Age

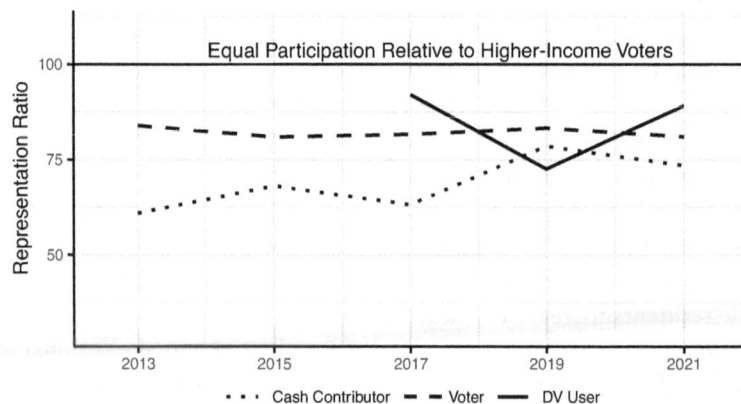

Figure 2.5c: Representation Ratios by Income

Figures 2.5: Representation Ratios of Democracy Voucher Users, Voters, and Cash Donors in Seattle Elections, 2013–2021

Finally, representation of lower-income Seattleites has increased markedly among democracy voucher users. Again, in this series we see a stark underrepresentation of lower-income Seattleites among cash donors before the program began. In 2013, lower-income individuals were 60 percent as likely as higher-income individuals to make a cash contribution, but about 80 percent as likely to vote. These representational disparities persist throughout the series. Among voucher users, however, the program has made substantial progress in broadening participation for lower-income residents, especially in 2017 and 2021. In these years, we see that democracy voucher users were closer to representational parity than even active voters. In other words, lower-income Seattleites were better represented among democracy voucher users than they were among active voters in 2017 and 2021.

Figures 2.5b and 2.5c illustrate another broad pattern in local participation. In tandem with the implementation of the Democracy Voucher program in Seattle, there has been a noticeable and significant increase in the representation of younger and lower-income citizens among cash donors. This trend may partly be explained by the large increases in small donations caused by the program itself.[26] As voters become more comfortable with this new form of participation, they may choose to "invest" some of their own money in local candidates in addition to using their vouchers. Other developments, such as the rise of internet fundraising, have likely played a role as well. Regardless of the exact cause of the trend, the pool of cash donors in Seattle has also diversified since 2017.

The Democracy Voucher program has thus dramatically increased representational equality in Seattle along lines of race, age, and class. When compared with cash donors to local elections before the program, democracy voucher users are more racially diverse, younger, and less affluent. Democracy voucher users much more closely resemble active voters, and, in some cases, voucher users are now more representative than even active voters themselves. Lower-income Seattleites and people of color were, in fact, better represented among voucher users than among voters in the municipal elections of 2021. Election cycle dynamics likely play a role in explaining some of this variation over time. Representational gains made during elections with citywide offices, like a competitive mayoral contest in 2021, may be harder to sustain during the relatively lower turnout elections for districted City Council seats (as in 2019). But that democracy voucher users were more representative than even active voters may also point to the efficacy of the program in another domain: empowering a wider pool of candidates to compete in local races, particularly in primary elections.

Participation, Renewal, and Representation for Local Candidates

In addition to broadening participation among Seattle voters, proponents of the Democracy Voucher program hoped that the program would empower more Seattleites to run for local office. Candidates with connections to affluent donors through personal or professional networks have a significant fundraising advantage, especially in the early months of a campaign.[27] This dynamic leaves less affluent, would-be candidates without a viable path to office. Without campaign funds, candidates lack the resources to hire staff, produce advertising materials to spread their message, and run a ground campaign to mobilize voters.[28] Because money is so critical to candidate success, it presents a high barrier to candidates without resources.

These fundraising barriers contribute to local elected officials across the nation being descriptively unlike the voters they represent. Local representatives are much whiter, wealthier, older, and more likely to be male than their constituents.[29] Descriptive representation, or the extent to which elected leaders resemble their constituents, is linked to higher levels of democratic legitimacy, a sense of efficacy for historically excluded groups, and better legislator–constituent relations.[30] The profound lack of descriptive representation in local governments imperils the connection of citizens to their elected leaders. At the same time, the exclusion of women, people of color, younger people, and the less affluent from local governments also translates into "profound and systematic biases" in policymaking.[31] Descriptive representation is important for both its symbolic impact and for the broader substantive effects on policy outcomes.

The Democracy Voucher program has created more opportunities for candidates to seek local office. The program has boosted candidate participation by creating fundraising opportunities for nontraditional candidates. In doing so, it opened the door for a new generation of Seattleites to serve in local government and may have consequently diversified the slate of elected officials. Although measuring the impact of these changes on policy outcomes is beyond the scope of our analysis, the results reported later in this chapter suggest that the program may be an important institutional pathway for increasing policy responsiveness in local governments.

Candidate Participation in the Democracy Voucher Program

The Democracy Voucher program has significantly reduced the barriers to candidate entry in local elections, thereby enabling a wider field of candidates to run for office. Since 2017, the program participation rate for candidates has consistently been high. Between 2017 and 2021, about 77 percent of primary election candidates and more than 80 percent of general election candidates have chosen to use the program to fund their campaigns.[32] The high candidate uptake rate underscores the allure of democratic fundraising for local campaigns. Thus far, only two nonparticipating candidates have won their general election bids, Kshama Sawant in 2019 (City Council District 3) and Sara Nelson in 2021 (at-large City Council). Sawant cited concerns about outside spending in her decision not to use the program, while Nelson voiced broad skepticism of the program's efficacy for engagement.[33]

One clear indication of the success of the program in attracting candidates is the sheer increase in the number of candidates running in Seattle municipal elections. Since the start of the program, the number of candidates has doubled over just three elections.[34] In the years between 2001 and 2016, Seattle's municipal elections saw, on average, about four candidates per race in the primary elections; after the program was introduced in 2017, that number doubled to about eight candidates per office. When compared to other similar cities in Washington and California, the number of candidates in Seattle elections has increased far beyond what we would expect from trends in local politics more generally.[35] Indeed, these rapid and dramatic increases in the size of the candidate pool speak to the program's deep efficacy in enabling more citizens to run for local office.

Interviews with former and current candidates show how the program has enabled nontraditional candidates to run for office in Seattle, regardless of their socioeconomic backgrounds.[36] Many of these candidates report that they would not have decided to run at all had the program not allowed them to collect democracy vouchers from everyday voters.[37] As one candidate attested:

> I think something that had stopped me from being a candidate in the past was this concept that you have to, like, self-finance your campaign. Like, I know people who ran before, and they re-financed their home. I was a renter. And there were no other renters on council. And I didn't have deep pockets. Right? My parents are . . . you know . . . strongly in the middle class, but they're public workers from a public university and worked for the state. So, it's not like I have the ability to self-finance a campaign or re-finance something as a renter. And democracy vouchers were coming out that year . . . So, I got into the race in 2017 in January. And in large part, it was because we had an opportunity to use those democracy vouchers.

And I saw it as a huge organizing tool to get people reengaged with democracy.

Other candidates echoed these sentiments but emphasized that the voters they hoped to serve while in office also lacked the resources to finance a successful political campaign. One candidate previously dismissed the idea of running for office because her "base is not wealthy." Through the program, the candidate was able to host a community campaign kick-off event in a lower-income immigrant community where she collected about 1,000 vouchers in one evening.

Candidates report using a wide variety of methods to collect democracy vouchers including direct door-to-door canvassing or "doorbelling" and "tabling" outside of busy community centers, including grocery stores and rail stations. They described hosting community events, such as barbeques, and collecting vouchers through social media solicitations. The promise of $100 in the hands of each voter in Seattle has incentivized candidates to interact directly with ordinary people. Indeed, a significant share of democracy vouchers is given directly to candidates each cycle, suggesting that the program is helping to focus candidate attention on future constituents.

The Democracy Voucher program has enabled ordinary Seattleites to seek local office by collecting vouchers from every corner of the city. The number of candidates in local races has doubled as public money has severed the dependence of candidates on networks of wealthy contributors. Most local candidates now use the program to run their campaigns, and they report using a wide variety of prodemocratic strategies to do so. Many of these strategies involve interacting directly with future constituents, pointing to the possibility that the program has opened new channels for underrepresented groups to communicate their needs and preferences to future policymakers.

Renewing the Pool of Local Candidates

The Democracy Voucher program has increased turnover in local office and enabled a new generation of candidates to compete in local elections. This has meant a decline in the so-called "incumbency advantage" that typically gives current officeholders an edge in competing for re-election.[38] By widening the sources of campaign cash, the program has also renewed the pool of local candidates in Seattle.

The effects of the program on renewing the candidate pool have been twofold. For one, the program has significantly decreased the percentage of incumbent local officeholders deciding to run for re-election. Between 2003 and 2016, about 78 percent of incumbents in Seattle chose to run for re-election to local office. After the program was implemented, that number plummeted by over 30 percentage points.[39] Second, incumbents face a tighter vote margin when they do decide to run. The final vote percentage received by incumbents dropped by nearly 18 percentage points in the elections after 2017, suggesting that quality challengers are being drawn into local races by the program.[40] Taken together, the evidence suggests that the Democracy Voucher program is effectively creating opportunities for a new generation of Seattleites to compete for local office.

Descriptive Representation in Seattle

The Democracy Voucher program may have also enabled a wider and more representative cross-section of Seattleites to run for local office. Table 2.2 provides a descriptive analysis of the demographic profiles of candidates in local elections both before and after the Democracy Voucher program was implemented. We look first at all Seattle candidates running for local office, then zoom in on City Council, mayoral, and winning (that is, those who won in the general election) candidates. We describe candidates' race, gender, and age.[41] Given the small number of candidates running for local offices in any election, we caution against reading too much into small fluctuations in candidate characteristics. Instead of emphasizing the magnitude of a particular change, we focus on the overall direction of the changes we observe with the introduction of the program. We also note that there could be other factors that have contributed to the changes in the candidate pool since 2017.

Table 2.2 shows a notable diversification of the candidate pool, particularly for mayoral and winning candidates. For city council and mayoral candidates combined, the percentage of women competing for local office increased and the mean age of local candidates has declined. In the pool of mayoral candidates, we see an increase in the percentages of people of color and women competing, suggesting that the program may be particularly helpful in supporting bids for the city's highest office. Candidates for the city's highest office were also, on average, younger after program implementation than before. There are also increases in the percentage of women and a decrease in the mean age of candidates seeking City Council seats. Curiously, the percentage of people of color competing for City Council remains virtually unchanged from the preprogram average.

The Democracy Voucher program is also associated with increases in the percentage of people of color and women among winning candidates. Notably, Seattle's local elected officeholders were quite racially and gender diverse before the program began, suggesting that other political and insti-

TABLE 2.2: CHARACTERISTICS OF THE LOCAL CANDIDATE POOL BEFORE AND AFTER THE DEMOCRACY VOUCHER PROGRAM (DVP)

	Before DVP	After DVP
All Candidates		
% People of Color	20.20	20.00
% Women	28.30	35.70
Mean Age in Years	51.09	47.32
Mayoral Candidates		
% People of Color	17.40	26.70
% Women	26.10	33.30
Mean Age in Years	54.61	50.40
City Council Candidates		
% People of Color	21.10	19.00
% Women	28.90	36.00
Mean Age in Years	50.03	46.86
Winning Candidates		
% People of Color	30.00	58.30
% Women	50.00	66.70
Mean Age in Years	54.55	46.58

tutional factors may be at play in Seattle. We also observe a substantial decrease in the mean age of winning candidates. Before the program, the average winning candidate was about fifty-five years old, similar to the national average of fifty-eight.[42] After program implementation, however, the average age decreased substantially, lowering the overall age of local officeholders by about eight years.

Democracy vouchers have helped empower more women and younger citizens to run for local office. Since 2017, the profile of local elected officials has shifted in a more egalitarian direction with a diverse City Council and mayor now serving the city. These changes suggest that this novel public campaign financing program may be a valuable institutional tool for enabling a wider array of candidates to run for office and, in so doing, increasing policy responsiveness on key local issues.[43]

Conclusion

When democracy reformers launched the Honest Elections campaign in late 2014, they envisioned a public campaign financing program that would make elections in Seattle more equitable. While they eventually settled on the Democracy Voucher program, they had no empirical evidence that the program would achieve its lofty goals. After all, as we described in the previous chapter, vouchers were merely an academic idea without any real-world data to prove their efficacy. Could they work? Could the program expand the donor pool, attract new contributors, and fight representational inequalities? Could this innovative public financing program attract new—and more—candidates who looked like the people they represent?

The program has shown a series of early successes in spurring voter participation, renewing the donor pool, and increasing representation of historically marginalized groups in the financing of local elections. Since 2017, the contribution rate in Seattle has leapfrogged over other major cities, making it a national leader in local donor participation. Compared to other cities that have, on average, contribution rates of 3 percent, Seattle's contributor rate stood at nearly 10 percent in 2021. At the same time, the donor pool in Seattle is now quite dynamic, drawing in thousands of new voucher participants each election cycle. Established cash donors are a small minority of the thousands of voters who finance Seattle elections. Although participation rates in the program remain uneven across sociodemographic groups, representational inequalities in Seattle have decreased. Voucher users are more representative than cash donors, particularly compared with cash donors before the program began. Overall, voucher users in Seattle look much more similar to active voters along lines of race, age, and income. In some cases, voucher users are closer to representational parity than voters themselves.

Our analyses indicate that participation, renewal, and representation have also increased for local candidates under the Democracy Voucher program, offering a potential pathway for more responsive local governance. Since 2017, the number of candidates in Seattle elections has exploded and the incumbency advantage has declined. Our preliminary analyses also offer hope that local candidates are becoming more diverse along lines of race, gender, and age. As the program matures, these outcomes will come into clearer focus and allow researchers to better measure the impact of the program on the quality of local governance. For now, we note strong descriptive evidence that the program is diversifying the candidate pool at the same time as it broadens voter participation in election financing.

Despite these impressive and rapid improvements, the Democracy Voucher program is not a cure for all that ails democracy at the local level. Representational inequalities in local politics have decreased under the program, but disparities in political voice persist. The remaining disparities in participation suggest that the voucher program is an effective policy tool, but it is not a panacea for the deeper, structural inequalities that animate American politics. Alongside public campaign finance, other reforms—like efforts to expand voter turnout in local elections and cultivate the local media ecosystem—may help support and supplement the important gains that the Democracy Voucher program has made.[44]

The clear successes of democracy vouchers have brought the program increasing national attention. While democratizing the campaign finance system, it has raised other concerns about the future of local democracy and the potential for the program's expansion beyond Seattle's city limits. In the next chapter, we turn our focus to the key challenges that face the program in Seattle and beyond. These challenges reflect both the practical realities of administering this novel program in a post–*Citizens United* age and the ongoing legal vulnerabilities that threaten the longevity of the program.

Change, Challenge, and Constitutional Controversy in Seattle

Despite significant progress over three election cycles, the Democracy Voucher program faces core challenges that threaten its legitimacy and longevity. Unpacking these challenges is important not only for the program in Seattle, but for opportunities to expand the program to other municipalities. As the residents of Seattle contemplate the reauthorization of the program, advocates from other cities, including Los Angeles and San Diego, are also considering adopting their own versions of the program. By identifying the key challenges to the Democracy Voucher program, both internally and externally, we consider what the future might hold for Seattle and how other cities can learn from Seattle in adopting their own version of the program.

The first set of challenges centers on program design, candidate practices, and administration by program managers. These internal challenges focus on the way political leaders design voucher programs, the way candidates participate in them, and the way program administrators adapt to shifting political circumstances. First, the successful design of a voucher program demands that local officials, acting in concert with administrators, consider difficult trade-offs between program participation, the value of the vouchers that voters receive, and total program costs. In Seattle, the Democracy Voucher program implemented spending caps for participating candidates to contain the costs of the program. This design choice, along with decisions about how many vouchers voters would receive and what those vouchers would be worth, ultimately constrains participation by residents.

As leaders in other municipalities contemplate program design, they will wrestle with this fundamental tension between program cost and resident participation.

Even a well-designed voucher program, like the one in Seattle, risks candidate engagement practices that strain, undermine, or even circumvent the intent of the program. Candidate strategies to maximize voucher collection may be at odds with the program's goals of building a more inclusive, engaged local democracy. In Seattle, candidates frequently employ data-driven campaigns that target highly engaged voters for outreach efforts. While helpful for efficiently collecting vouchers, this practice may leave behind residents in the more marginal communities the program was intended to mobilize. Finally, the implementation of the Democracy Voucher program underscores the complex, time-consuming nature of administering public campaign financing programs. The experience of administrators in Seattle highlights the importance of rapid, adaptive responses to maintaining the viability and legitimacy of this novel program.

While internal challenges can be managed by thoughtful program design and administration, the most serious threats to this form of public financing are external to the program. First Amendment–based legal challenges imperil the future of the program in Seattle, as well as the legitimacy of the core voucher concept itself. These challenges to the program take two forms. On one hand, direct attacks to the program's legal basis jeopardize the standing of the program in Seattle, and threaten the legality of public campaign financing programs more generally. On the other hand, the proliferation of independent expenditures—spending by outside groups uncoordinated with candidate campaigns—creates indirect threats to the program. Independent expenditures have risen faster in Seattle than in several other cities in Washington, suggesting that the program may have spurred external spending. There are no easy solutions to these challenges. The future of public campaign financing—and particularly, the opportunity to expand the voucher concept beyond Seattle—hinges on maintaining high rates of candidate participation even in the face of outside spending.

These issues are also important for the longevity of the program in Seattle. The program will soon reach the end of its ten-year tax levy and require reauthorization. In 2025, voters in Seattle will consider whether to refund the program. But there is much more at stake than the future of Seattle's program. Municipalities across the country are considering programs modeled on the experience of Seattle. In 2021, the U.S. House of Representatives passed a proposal for a pilot national voucher program, although the bill did not become law. The voucher model has the potential to transform the way American elections are funded, but understanding—and resolving—both the practical and legal challenges will be essential to that transformation.

Internal Challenges of Design, Participation, and Administration

Seattle's novel experiment with democracy vouchers has brought to light a set of internal program challenges. These challenges reflect the difficulty in—and ambiguity of—adapting an ambitious and far-reaching public campaign finance program for use by actual localities. Municipalities, including Seattle, often juggle budgetary priorities as they contend with concerns around public health, safety, and development. We identify three broad internal areas of challenge as Seattle has brought this novel program to life: program *design*, *practice*, and *administration*. These issue areas are fundamental to understanding how the program works both in principle and in practice.

Balancing Cost and Participation in Program Design

Designing the Democracy Voucher program required policymakers and program administrators to consider tradeoffs between controlling election costs, maximizing voter participation, and sustaining high candidate uptake rates. When legal scholars first conceptualized the democracy dollars program, they envisioned giving each American voter a redeemable coupon or debit card that could be used to finance candidates running for national office. The only constraint on the amount of money that a candidate could collect from voters would be their fundraising ability. Candidates would be awash in cash as a sea of democracy dollars stretched before them.

In Seattle, this idealized version of the program ran up against practical constraints. The Democracy Voucher program was funded by a ten-year dedicated property tax levy that set hard limits on the total amount the new program could spend. To ensure that the program stayed within these funding limits, local officials adopted spending limits for each eligible city office. As we showed in Chapter 2, these limits determine how much a participating candidate can spend during each phase of the election. By mandating spending caps for each office, Seattle policymakers aimed to reign in the overall costs of the program and level the playing field for participating candidates. While this important design choice ensured the viability of the inaugural program, it also had consequences for both voters and candidates participating in the program. For voters, the spending caps in place for each office set an upper limit on the overall voucher redemption rate and, in turn, on the overall participation rate for an election cycle. For instance, in a districted City Council election featuring four qualified candidates in each district the maximum number of voucher users—in the primary and general elections combined—would be about 33,000. In turn, the highest potential participation rate in the program for that cycle would be about 6.56 percent.[1] This redemption rate is still much higher than the contributor rate in other cities around the country (see Figure 2.2). However, the rate is also far lower than other forms of participation, such as voting. To critics, the low redemption rate compromises the impact of the program by excluding a large portion of the Seattle electorate each cycle.

In Seattle, limiting the maximum voucher redemption rate for participants may have another unintended consequence. By setting a ceiling for voucher redemption in each cycle, the program's representational gains among people of color and younger and lower-income voters may be harder to sustain. As we demonstrated in the last chapter, program participation rates were lower in the districted elections of 2019 compared to the competitive 2021 citywide races. This pattern may become cyclical, with higher voucher redemption rates in costlier, citywide elections and lower rates in less expensive districted races. Importantly, representational disparities tend to increase when participation rates are lower, suggesting that cycles with lower maximum participation may yield larger representational disparities.[2] The program's long-term success may, in part, hinge on finding ways to increase engagement in the lower-stakes districted council elections cycles and to maintain representational gains across cycles.

Spending caps in Seattle also gave rise to the so-called "wasted voucher" problem. Each cycle, candidates can redeem vouchers assigned to them only until they have reached the spending cap for their office (see Table 2.1). Voters may not realize that candidates reached their spending caps, and they may assign their vouchers to candidates who cannot redeem them. This is the "wasted vouchers" problem. In 2017, 29 percent of vouchers were assigned to a qualified campaign but never redeemed because the candidate had already reached the applicable voucher maximum.[3] Under the rules of the program, vouchers cannot be reallocated once they are assigned to a candidate. This dynamic may deter voters from participating in the program in subsequent cycles if they believe their vouchers will not be redeemed. Voters might perceive that participation is a "waste" if their preferred candidates can no longer redeem vouchers. Nonetheless, even when vouchers cannot be redeemed, the act of assigning a voucher may help voters feel more invested in a local candidate and the outcome of local elections, thereby contributing to the broader goals of the program.

One potential solution to the "wasted voucher" problem is to change the number of vouchers provided to residents or the monetary value of those vouchers. In Seattle, residents receive four vouchers worth $25 each. By changing either the number of vouchers received by voters or the value of each voucher, program administrators could expand opportunities for Seattle residents to participate in the program. For example, they could reduce the number of vouchers sent to each voter. If voters received only two vouchers, each of which was valued at $25, the maximum participation rate for any election would double, relative to the current system. Another possibility is that the number and value of vouchers be pegged to the spending caps in place for that election. Voters could be sent fewer vouchers (or less valuable vouchers) during districted elections than during citywide contests.

Lowering the total cash value of the democracy vouchers may seem like an attractive way to increase program participation, but doing so may simultaneously dampen candidate enthusiasm. As the value of the vouchers decreases for each voter, the time and efficiency costs of running a voucher campaign would increase for candidates. Putting less valuable vouchers in the hands of voters could depress candidate buy-in to the program and make voucher collection less attractive compared to cash contributions. This is especially true if the program's spending caps are raised in future cycles to reflect rising campaign costs.[4]

In designing public campaign finance programs, policymakers are often forced to make trade-offs between controlling costs and sustaining candidate (and voter) participation. In the context of democracy vouchers, these policy decisions are particularly vexing and acute given the novelty of the program. With only one existing model to use as a template, policymakers will have to make complex design choices that bear directly on voter and candidate participation in local elections. To help aid decision-making, policymakers should simulate the anticipated costs of their local races with several plausible voucher denominations that allow for different levels of voucher redemption rates. Here, municipalities might also consider whether the number and value of vouchers should be modulated to the slate of offices eligible for the program each cycle.

Program Practice: Constraining Candidate Strategies

While the Democracy Voucher program has transformed local elections by changing the people who fund elections, it has also led to a meaningful transformation in the candidates seeking local office.[5] As we noted in the previous chapter, the program has resulted in notable increases in the diversity of candidates and elected officials. About 80 percent of candidates participated in the Democracy Voucher program in each of the last three election cycles, underscoring the appeal of a well-funded public finance program for local elections. As we noted, the program has also increased the number of candidates running for each office. Each race in Seattle now features an average of about eight candidates in the primary elections.[6]

On the flip side, skeptics of the program have warned about the program attracting too many candidates each cycle, leading to confusion or even disinterest among voters. Critics worry that the quality of candidates seeking elective office has decreased as the number of candidates has ballooned.[7] With a growing slate of candidates, voters may experience confusion in selecting between options in primary elections. The "paradox of choice" describes the general condition of having too many equivalent options, leading to fatigue or indifference.[8] With a widening candidate pool in local elections, Seattle voters may choose to retreat from local contests as the information costs of candidate selection increase, rather than engaging with the political process.[9]

Beyond the challenges of larger slates of candidates, the strategies used by these candidates to collect vouchers have broad implications for the impact of the program. As noted in the previous chapter, the Democracy Voucher program sets qualifying requirements and limits the amount of money that candidates can collect. But beyond these program rules, candidates have relatively wide latitude in deciding how to collect vouchers, where to focus those collection efforts, and how much to rely on vouchers in their electoral strategy. As candidates develop their own internal strategies for running a voucher-financed campaign, their plans have important implications for voter participation.

The architects of the Democracy Voucher program envisioned local candidates interacting with their constituents to collect vouchers. By encouraging that interaction, the program would expand the range of perspectives heard by candidates on the campaign trail. While these interactions would serve as a conduit for voter concerns, they would also integrate marginalized community members into local politics. But in practice, candidate strategies often emphasize efficiency in the collection of vouchers, thereby bypassing these organic interactions altogether. For instance, candidates report that "doorbelling" is a common method of collecting democracy vouchers. Candidates and their campaign representatives choose a particular neighborhood and go door to door to introduce themselves, talk about their campaigns, and collect democracy vouchers. On the surface, "doorbelling" is precisely the type of interaction between candidate and constituent that the program was designed to foster. During the 2019 elections, about a quarter of Seattle residents reported that they had had a campaign representative knock on their door, and about 11 percent of Seattleites had a candidate appear at their door.[10]

At the same time, candidates also report that this strategy may leave behind harder-to-reach populations and disadvantaged communities. In fact, only a small minority of campaigns in 2019 reported significant efforts to mobilize harder-to-reach and less engaged communities.[11] This is especially true in communities with high concentrations of foreign-born residents, where language and cultural barriers pose additional hurdles to voucher collection. Candidates report spending additional time and effort in these communities to explain the program and allay concerns about providing personal information to the city.[12] Candidate strategies that avoid marginalized communities or difficult-to-reach populations jeopardize the program's commitment to spurring political participation and reducing representational disparities in local elections.

While candidates may not actively avoid harder-to-reach communities, their data-driven campaign strategies to micro-target highly engaged "likely voters" may reproduce some of the inequalities of a cash system. Many modern political campaigns use voter outreach software that allows campaign staff to identify the voters who are most likely to vote in an election.[13] Although targeting these voters for vouchers may yield gains in efficiency, the strategy may leave behind less engaged voters who have not historically been active in local politics. Highly engaged voters more closely approximate traditional campaign donors than the "ordinary" residents that the program aims to mobilize. The consequences of these micro-targeting strategies represent "grey areas" for the Democracy Voucher program. These strategies certainly do not constitute candidate misconduct, but they skirt the intention of the program. The ways candidates adapt their voucher collection strategies to the realities of running a modern campaign are not easily addressed by additional program rules or requirements.

While micro-targeting as a campaign strategy undermines the ability of the program to broaden participation, concerns about outright fraud pose another serious threat to the integrity of Seattle's program. To date, there has been only one suspected case of candidate fraud in Seattle. In 2017, a candidate for City Council was accused of falsifying donor records and using personal funds to meet the program's qualification threshold.[14] The candidate later faced criminal charges and agreed to forty-eight hours of community service for the offense. Importantly, the incident brought early attention to the potential for fraud, despite the significant safeguards in place to prevent misconduct.[15]

More recently, a mayoral candidate's campaign in 2021 pushed the limits of the program with a scheme to "harvest" vouchers through an army of paid staff contracted through a political consultant. The hired staff used voucher replacement forms, which are meant as a convenience to voters who have misplaced their democracy vouchers before assigning them, to collect vouchers en masse from voters. The staff deceived voters by claiming that the signed vouchers would be used to address the city's growing homelessness problem, hiding the fact that they were being used to support the candidate's campaign.[16] On Election Day, the candidate's campaign garnered more democracy vouchers than votes, raising questions about the integrity of the voucher collection system itself.[17]

The success of the voucher program in attracting a wide field of candidates injects a significant amount of complexity into races for local office. From the perspective of the voter, the increase in electoral competition may appear as an additional time and information cost to bear in an off-year election. For candidates, translating voucher collection into a viable campaign strategy may strain, undermine, or even circumvent the original intent of the program. These are not problems that lend themselves to a policy correction per se. Instead, policymakers and program administrators should be aware of how on-the-ground practices depart from principle and adapt their outreach and education efforts in tandem.

Program Administration: Costs and Adaptation

The Democracy Voucher program also comes with considerable administrative costs and challenges. At the most basic level, the administrative costs of running the program include printing vouchers, mailing them to voters, and staffing the program. In Seattle, the Democracy Voucher program has a small standing staff to oversee the program, collect and disseminate program data, train and educate local candidates, and spearhead voter education efforts. During local election years, program administrators hire a significant temporary staff to process the vouchers and ensure the timely distribution of funds to local candidates. For each voucher that is returned, the staff must (1) verify that the returned voucher originated from a registered Seattle voter or qualified resident; (2) validate the signature on a returned voucher; (3) track the status of each voucher in a database for public dissemination; and (4) distribute public monies to candidates. To verify voter signatures, the program contracts with the King County Board of Elections, which maintains official voter records.

The program's overall administrative costs have averaged about $800,000 per year since 2017. In comparison to the city budget of $7 billion (in 2023), administering the voucher program is a tiny expense amounting to about .01 percent of the annual city budget. Nevertheless, the cost of administration is comparable to administering other critical city services, including outreach to unhoused people living in street encampments, HIV management programs, and improvements to the city's street safety.[18] Spending on elections can become quite controversial in tighter budgetary climates, when elected officials must weigh the value of this funding against these other crucial programs. Since the Seattle program is currently funded through a ten-year tax levy, it is temporarily insulated from year-to-year budgetary fights. However, as we note later, these cost and benefit calculations may be salient to the program's levy renewal.

The experience of Seattle also underscores the importance of coordination and nimble adaptation to respond to a changing political environment.[19] Program administrators in Seattle work for the Seattle Ethics and Elections Committee (SEEC) to regulate campaigns and elections, including the rules of campaign finance programs. Since the program launched, program administrators, under the direction of the SEEC, have adapted the program to the ongoing threat of outside spending. They have also streamlined the candidate qualification process, updated program guidelines to prevent voucher harvesting, increased spending caps for eligible city offices, and quickly adjusted the program in the face of the COVID-19 pandemic.[20] While the basic design of the democracy voucher program is written into the city's municipal code, program administrators must nimbly respond to a host of unpredictable developments in the local political ecosystem.

The program will reach the end of its initial funding period in 2025. While program administrators built the Democracy Voucher program from scratch and deftly adapted the program to changing political winds, the future of the program is out of their control. The fate of the program lies with Seattle voters, who must balance the city's many competing—and costly—priorities. There is a possibility that the program will be jettisoned to conserve limited city funds for other contentious and highly visible social issues in Seattle, including public safety, housing affordability, and homelessness.[21] The program is a small expense in the overall city budget, but public campaign finance often faces significant headwinds when the political or economic climate sours.[22] If voters decline to fund the program, Seattle could lose the considerable administrative expertise and insight that went into launching and building the nation's first experiment with democracy vouchers.

External Challenges: Constitutional Legitimacy and Independent Expenditures

The most fundamental threats to the program's longevity stem from First Amendment challenges to public campaign financing. These challenges draw on a long legal history that equates some forms of campaign spending with political speech. These First Amendment challenges take two forms. First, the program in Seattle has invited direct legal challenges on grounds that Democracy Vouchers infringe on the free speech rights of the property owners who pay for the program. Second, the Supreme Court's classification of independent campaign expenditures as protected political speech has opened the door for outside spending in Seattle elections. This flood of outside spending has largely come from wealthy donors and organized interests, undermining the intent of the program to amplify the voices of ordinary voters.

Direct Legal Challenges

The U.S. Supreme Court sanctioned the use of public campaign financing in American elections in a landmark 1976 case, *Buckley v. Valeo*, but the unique structure of the Democracy Voucher program in Seattle has provoked new, targeted challenges. Funds for the program come from a ten-year tax levy on Seattle property owners. Funding derived from this so-called "earmarked tax," rather than tax dollars from general funds, has invited new legal scrutiny about whether the Democracy Voucher program amounts to compelled political speech.

The first legal challenge to the program was brought by two Seattle property owners, Mark Elster and Sarah Pynchon, in late 2017. In *Elster v. City of Seattle*, the plaintiffs' complaint alleged that the program infringed on their First Amendment rights by using taxpayer dollars to fund speech that they did not support. In legal terms, they argued that the Democracy Voucher program infringed on First Amendment rights because it "unconstitutionally compel[led] them to support the program's message."[23]

The case was first brought to King County Superior Court in 2017, where the court granted the city's motion to dismiss.[24] Elster and Pynchon appealed the decision to the Washington State Supreme Court, where the case was heard in 2019. The Washington State Supreme Court unanimously ruled in favor of Seattle and rejected the claim that the program infringed on First Amendment rights. In its opinion, the court argued that the tax levied on Seattle property owners "does not alter, abridge, restrict, censor or burden speech" and that property owners were not "individually associate[d] . . . with any message conveyed by the Democracy Voucher program."[25] Instead, the majority cited the precedent set in *Buckley* to argue that the tax and the program support public debate and participation in elections.[26] In March 2020, the U.S. Supreme Court declined to hear the case, leaving the Washington State Supreme Court's decision to stand.[27]

Although the Washington State Supreme Court's unanimous decision in 2019 put Seattle's Democracy Voucher program on firmer legal ground, it remains an open question whether other courts—including the U.S. Supreme Court—would come to the same conclusion. Seattle's unique funding mechanism—a tax levied on local property owners and specifically earmarked for the program—opened the door to legal challenges. Even if the Seattle program were funded through general tax revenues, rather than an "earmarked" tax, public campaign financing could be in jeopardy if the Supreme Court revisits its long-standing precedent set in *Buckley.* Given other recent campaign finance rulings, such as *Citizens United v. FEC*, public campaign financing at large could be at risk if the court's conservative majority reasons that *all* taxpayer-funded political speech runs afoul of the First Amendment.[28]

Independent Expenditures

While legal challenges may chip away at the legitimacy of the Democracy Voucher program, independent expenditures by outside groups pose the most intractable and immediate threat. An independent expenditure is campaign spending made to influence an election or support a candidate. An independent *expenditure* is different from a *contribution* made directly to a campaign committee.[29] The distinction between a contribution and an expenditure dates back to the critical 1976 Supreme Court case, *Buckley v. Valeo.* In its decision, the court held that while campaign contributions could be limited, campaign expenditures were "core political speech" that could not.[30]

In setting the broad legal parameters for regulating money in politics, *Buckley v. Valeo* hamstrung efforts to limit the amount of money that can be independently spent on political campaigns by private individuals.[31] In 2010, the Supreme Court's decision in *Citizens United v. FEC* extended this right to spend independently in elections to corporations and unions.[32] For instance, corporations can now use their general treasury funds to produce and air television advertisements in support of candidates so long as those advertisements are not made in coordination with candidates' political campaigns. These independent forms of campaign spending can take many forms, including mailers to voters highlighting a particular issue, television advertisements that support (or oppose) a candidate, and get-out-the-vote activities. While these activities must be uncoordinated with candidate campaigns, this standard has been difficult to define and defend in practice.

Most independent expenditures are now made through special independent expenditure-only committees, more commonly known as "super PACs." These committees are the most important consequence of the decision *Citizens United v. FEC* in conjunction with a subsequent lower-court decision, *SpeechNow.org v. FEC*. Super PACs can collect donations of unlimited size from private citizens, corporations, and labor unions and pool these donations to make independent expenditures.[33] In essence, super PACs allow individuals, corporations, and unions to finance independent campaign spending—such as television advertisements or a mailer attacking a candidate—without having to produce the activity themselves.[34] In recent elections, super PACs have become ever more important players in federal, state, and, notably, local elections.[35]

Independent expenditures made by super PACs in local elections imperil the Democracy Voucher program on multiple levels. For one, the ever-present threat of spending by outside groups may make the spending caps associated with program participation less attractive to potential candidates. In the long term, this may undermine candidate participation in the program. When the Democracy Voucher program was designed, the spending caps were designed to both ensure that the program remained affordable to administer and even the playing field for participating candidates. But if candidates routinely contend with multi-million-dollar independent expenditures orchestrated by local interest groups, the program could become untenable as candidates begin to view the spending caps as too restrictive and logistically onerous.

Independent expenditures have also strained program resources and demanded nimble responses from program administrators. If a participating candidate can show that one or more of her opponents has benefitted from outside spending in excess of the program's spending cap, the candidate may petition to be released from the limit. Once a candidate is released from these spending caps, they can collect cash contributions beyond the initial spending limit, although the cap on vouchers remains. For instance, a candidate running for mayor can ordinarily collect up to $400,000 in vouchers for their primary campaign. If an opponent's campaign receives support from an outside group in the form of independent expenditures totaling $500,000, the candidate is released from the spending caps and may collect cash contributions beyond the $400,000 limit.[36]

Adapting program rules to the realities of independent expenditures also requires a robust, efficient disclosure regime to guide decision-making. Disclosure regimes are the laws, rules, and practices that determine how political committees report their campaign contributions and expenditures. Once this information is disclosed, it is typically made available to the public. Disclosure acts as a significant source of information about who finances candidates and committees. It also allows policymakers to enforce campaign laws.[37]

In Seattle, committees that finance independent expenditures are required to report their activity to the SEEC. The disclosure guidelines are quite stringent. They require a report if the committee spends more than $100 on an expenditure targeting a single candidate or $200 in contributions or expenditures in a reporting period. Each disclosure report to the SEEC contains basic information about the sponsor of an independent expenditure, its amount, and the date of the expenditure. The beneficiary (or target) of the independent expenditure is also included in the disclosure filing so that program administrators—and the public—can track outside spending in support of or in opposition to a local candidate.

While independent expenditures create practical strains that amplify the burdens of program administrators, they may imperil the legitimacy of the program in the eyes of voters. The Democracy Voucher program was designed, in part, to reduce the reliance of candidates on large donors dominating local politics. However, if the program itself stimulates outside spending through independent expenditures, it may have the effect of simply transforming the nature of those large donations, rather than decreasing their influence altogether. Since the program sets stringent contribution limits and gives voice to average voters, it may also incentivize wealthy residents and interest groups to rely on other mechanisms to leverage their influence in local elections. Against its original intent, the program may indirectly erode the quality of local democracy by forcing big money to use less regulated means to influence elections.

To the extent that the Democracy Voucher program is driving outside spending in Seattle elections, the level of independent expenditures in Seattle would be expected to rise more quickly than in other cities without public campaign financing programs. Figure 3.1 shows the per capita independent expenditures made in local elections in Seattle and five large cities in Washington. The figure should be interpreted with some caution. Although the scale of independent expenditures has been adjusted for population size, there are many other salient differences between cities that are not captured. The figure is meant to provide a preliminary snapshot of indepen-

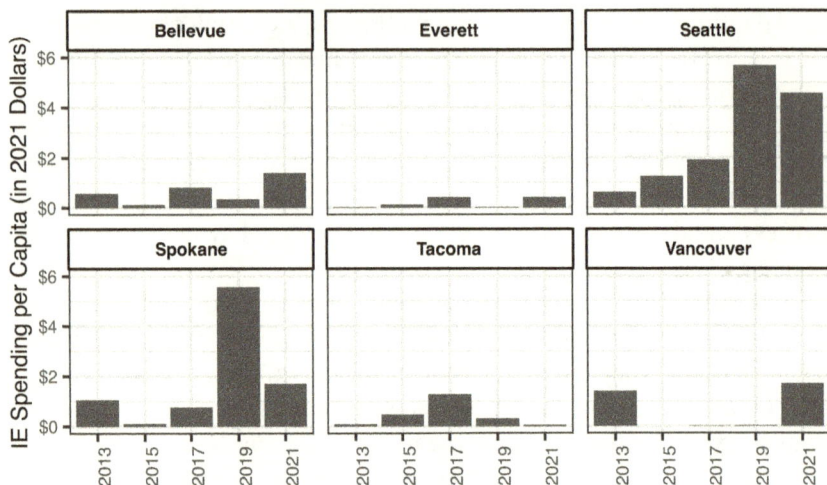

Figure 3.1: Per Capita Spending on Independent Expenditures (2021 Dollars) in Local Elections across Major Cities in Washington State, 2013–2021

dent expenditures in local elections around Washington State, rather than identifying the primary cause of these differences across places.

The growth of independent expenditures in local elections is not unique to Seattle, but it is most pronounced there. From 2013 to 2021, independent expenditures did increase in other cities, including Spokane and Bellevue, although the increases were not as dramatic or consistent as those in Seattle. Compared to 2013, independent expenditures in Seattle exploded in 2019 and 2021 on a per capita basis. The most notable increase occured in 2019, when independent expenditures per capita more than tripled from the previous election cycle.

In the 2019 elections, which featured the seven districted City Council races with three of the seven seats open, outside groups spent over $4 million to influence contests in several districts. The most prolific spender in the 2019 election was a business-backed outside group called Civic Alliance for a Sound Economy (CASE), organized by the Seattle Metropolitan Chamber of Congress. More than half of CASE's money was donated by Amazon after a public fight with the sitting council over a new tax on high-grossing Seattle companies.[38] Although Amazon had long called Seattle home, it had not previously been a visible participant in local elections.[39] In response to the explosion in large donations to super PACs in 2019, the Seattle City Council passed a measure in early 2020 that prohibited "foreign-influenced" corporations from donating to super PACs in local elections.[40] The measure successfully reigned in large corporations like Amazon, but smaller local businesses have nonetheless stepped in to fund outside campaigns, including in 2021.

Growing media attention to the role of outside spending in the 2019 and 2021 elections helped fuel a narrative linking the explosion in independent expenditures to the Democracy Voucher program itself. While there appears to be some truth to this narrative, the program's role in fueling the rise in outside spending may be mediated by the increase in electoral competition in local elections, as we noted in Chapter 2. The program has significantly decreased the incumbency advantage in local races, compared with other cities in Washington. This has translated into substantially fewer incumbents deciding to run again for local office and more candidates overall. More open seats and more competition for previously "safe" seats from voucher-financed challengers may drive outside spending directly.[41] In 2019, for instance, three of seven incumbents in districted City Council seats ran for re-election, leaving the remaining four seats open. This pattern is on par with postprogram averages for electoral competition in Seattle. In federal races, independent expenditures tend to cluster in competitive contests.[42] This pattern makes sense, since outside groups target races where their spending is likely to have the most impact.

Even if the rise of independent expenditures by outside groups is mediated by the increase in electoral competition in local races, the effect may be the same. Independent expenditures may erode candidate participation in the program. The system of public campaign financing for presidential elections is an instructive case in point. Put in place in 1974, the presidential campaign financing program allotted public funds for both the nomination and general election campaigns. Until the early 2000s, all Democratic and Republican presidential candidates had used this system of public financing.[43] In 2000, presidential candidate George W. Bush made national headlines for declining matching funds during the nomination period, fearing that his self-financed opponent, Steve Forbes, would greatly outspend him.[44] The 2004 presidential election saw increased spending by outside groups financed by unlimited donations.[45] In 2008, Barack Obama became the first major party nominee since 1976 to ever decline public funds in both the nomination *and* general elections, telling his supporters in a video message that the public system was "broken."[46]

This dynamic whereby escalating outside spending undermines the value of public funding to candidates has led to questions about the efficacy of *any* effort to stem the tide of money in politics. In the so-called hydraulic view of money in politics, "political money, like water, has to go somewhere" and reforms intended to cap election expenditures simply redirect the flow of money to other outlets (i.e., outside spending of whatever form).[47] By displacing money that might otherwise be channeled to candidates or parties, expenditure limitations push money into conduits lacking institutional buffers and undermine the intent of reform.[48] This dynamic did, indeed, play out in the context of presidential financing where candidates were constrained by expenditure limitations and outside groups stepped into the void. Today, the presidential system of public campaign financing is no longer used by major party candidates because the program's limitations are viewed as too onerous and its benefits too few.[49] This dynamic could easily play out in Seattle if independent expenditures change the calculus of program participation for local candidates.

Seattle has already adopted several reforms to mitigate the impact of independent expenditures on candidate participation. The SEEC continues to review and honor requests from candidates to be released from the program's spending limits when faced with an independent expenditure-backed opponent. This stopgap measure will likely continue to be utilized in local races and especially in competitive citywide races. So far, the threat of independent expenditures has dissuaded only one candidate from participating in the program, and rates of candidate uptake remain high. The current legal landscape constrains the options available to policymakers in Seattle and all but guarantees that independent expenditures will continue to affect local races if the program is renewed.

Looking Forward

After three election cycles, Seattle's pioneering Democracy Voucher program has spurred participation in local elections, diversified the donor pool, and attracted more candidates for local office. Yet, it has also created new challenges for the system of public campaign finance. Several of those concerns reflect internal issues endemic to the design of the program, its utilization by local candidates, and management by program administrators. Wrestling with these types of issues is inherent to all public financing programs, including the more common matching programs described in Chapter 1, but they are particularly acute in a new program like the Democracy Voucher program, where no playbook exists to guide decision-making. As the idea for a voucher program spreads beyond Seattle, local political leaders and program administrators will need to grapple with similar program design issues that simultaneously balance program costs, candidate engagement, and citizen participation. Without question, the lessons learned from Seattle will prove instructive in future program design.

These internal, practical challenges are no doubt important, but they are secondary to a more existential legal threat to the idea of a voucher program. As the program expands to other jurisdictions—and one day, possibly to a national program—new legal challenges are likely to follow. Although a case about the program has not yet been heard in the U.S. Supreme Court, it is very possible that a majority-conservative court will find aspects of the program objectionable.

Ultimately, the most serious and immediate threat to the Democracy Voucher program is the rapid rise of independent expenditures by outside groups. Under the current legal framework, local policymakers and administrators lack any viable option to curtail these expenditures in local elections. While Seattle officials have adapted the program to deal with this threat, we expect that outside spending by super PACs will continue to challenge the viability of the program. The success of all public campaign financing programs depends on maintaining candidate participation and ensuring program legitimacy in the eyes of voters. That a program designed to transform the system of money in politics may, in fact, lead to a greater role for the wealthy and organized interests remains a core threat to public financing.

Despite these issues and challenges, there is enthusiasm for expanding on the model pioneered in Seattle. In the Conclusion, we point to other movements in Oakland, Los Angeles, and San Diego working to build on the success of Seattle. Although advocates in these cities are only beginning the process of constructing political coalitions to support innovative public financing programs, they offer a hopeful sign that the Seattle model will spread beyond the Emerald City, transforming the way municipal elections are funded across the country.

Conclusion

Democracy Vouchers and the Future
of American Elections

After nearly a decade, Seattle's experiment with the Democracy Voucher program stands at a crossroads. On one hand, the program successfully spurred participation and broadened the pool of contributors in local elections. Candidates winning elective office are more diverse than ever, since the program has opened new opportunities to raise money across the city. Program administrators have addressed many challenges to create a successful, well-managed program in Seattle. In light of these successes, Seattle's experiment with the voucher program offers a viable reform to strengthen local, state, and even national democracy.

Despite these clear successes, several lingering concerns cast doubt on the program's future. Chief among these concerns is the dramatic rise in outside spending in Seattle elections. Although this spending may be driven by increased competition in local elections, the specter of this form of spending may eclipse its strong gains in other areas. Whether or not the program's rapid participatory and representational gains can offset the perilous rise in outside spending is an open question. Likewise, whether this campaign finance system can move the needle on local policy outcomes and disrupt entrenched patterns of urban inequality remains to be seen.

While voters in Seattle will need to reauthorize funding for the Democracy Voucher program to continue the program beyond 2025, the broader future of this innovative reform is at a crossroads, too. Policy innovations in a single city often spur emulators across municipalities, especially as evidence suggests that program innovations effectively contribute to the resolution of complex social problems. But although the Democracy Voucher program has taken root in the culture of Seattle politics, its proliferation beyond Seattle has been slow. Building from the analysis throughout the book, we address the diffusion of this reform later in this conclusion, where we consider challenges and opportunities to push beyond Seattle to adopt a publicly financed voucher program more broadly.

Summing Up

In 2015, Seattle became the first municipality to pass the transformative democracy dollars model of public campaign financing. Chapter 1 describes how this innovative idea gained momentum in Seattle. On the heels of a narrow defeat to create a public matching program in local elections, a coalition of strong civic organizations and local activists seized a political opportunity to build a movement for wider reform. The newly energized coalition regrouped around the idea of a democracy dollars program to strengthen the connection of voters to local politics and give them a voice in selecting local candidates early in the campaign season. The coalition mounted a campaign for a ballot initiative called the Honest Election Seattle Initiative (I-122). The initiative packaged the idea of a novel public campaign finance program with a slate of good government reforms. In November 2015, I-122 was approved with 63 percent of voters in support of the effort, making Seattle the first locality in the nation to pass this radical new program.

Starting in 2017, registered voters in Seattle now receive four $25 democracy vouchers to allocate to eligible local candidates, alleviating the monetary burden of contributing for average voters and supplying local candidates with a wide potential base of financial support to run their campaigns. In Chapter 2, we show that participation in Seattle's local elections has exploded. Today, the city boasts one of the highest contributor rates in the country. At the same time, the program has broadly diversified the donor pool along lines of race, age, and income. We see these patterns among local candidates as well. The number of candidates in local races has doubled while the incumbency advantage has markedly declined. This wider pool of candidates has translated into elected officials who are, on average, younger and include more people of color and women. Chapter 2 carefully details these key successes of the voucher program over the last three election cycles.

But the program has not been without its challenges. Alongside these positive developments, the Democracy Voucher program confronts a set of internal and external threats that call into question the future of the program in Seattle. As the program nears the renewal date for its dedicated property tax levy, policymakers and voters alike will need to address these challenges. There are no easy policy solutions for these internal obstacles, but the playbook in Seattle provides critical insights for other municipalities on the verge of adopting the program. First, the design of a voucher program demands careful attention to the difficult trade-offs between containing election costs and maximizing participation in the program. While these trade-offs are not unique to the voucher program, they are particularly acute in the context of this innovative participation-centered approach. Second, candidate practices in collecting vouchers can deviate in important ways from the ideals of program designers. By targeting already highly engaged communities to maximize efficiency, candidates may undermine the intent of the voucher model to better integrate historically marginalized communities into the fabric of local politics. Finally, the experience in Seattle underscores the extent to which effective program administration demands nimble, adaptive responses from administrators and a robust disclosure regime to guide decision-making.

Most pressingly, First Amendment challenges constitute an existential threat to the program. We identify two ways these legal challenges imperil the voucher design. First, direct legal challenges to the program are likely to crop up as more localities adopt the program for their elections. Eventually, a case about the program could be heard in the U.S. Supreme Court, where a conservative majority could overturn the affirmation of public campaign financing set forth in *Buckley*.[1] Finally, we show that independent expenditures have grown at a rapid clip in Seattle elections, surpassing the growth in independent expenditures in other major cities in Washington. That the program itself may beget this type of outside spending risks the legitimacy of the program in the eyes of voters, complicates program administration, and channels big political money through less regulated conduits.

Looking Beyond Seattle: Democracy Vouchers on the Move

The success of the Democracy Voucher program in broadening participation in local elections has earned the program increasing interest from reformers in other cities. As local political leaders and activists seek to reform elections and fight money in politics, several have given a close look to the experience in Seattle. In several cities, including Los Angeles and San Diego, political leaders are currently considering adoption of the voucher model for their city elections. At the same time, a handful of states have considered bills to bring vouchers to state elections. Since Seattle has wrestled with core programmatic and administrative challenges, these movements are all turning to Seattle as a blueprint for improving the quality of local democracy in their own jurisdictions. They have also looked to Seattle for lessons about the unintended consequences of implementing a largely effective program that could upset the balance of power in local elections.

Municipal and State Movements

In 2022, voters in Oakland, California, approved the nation's second democracy voucher program. At the polls, voters overwhelmingly approved Ballot Measure W, known as the Oakland Fair Elections Act, to bring the democracy voucher program to citywide elections. The program was modeled closely on the experience of Seattle.[2]

While voters offered overwhelming support for the program, the program's implementation was postponed almost as soon as it was passed. In 2023, the mayor's budget stripped the program of its first round of anticipated funding, leaving the fate of the program in limbo as elected officials grapple with competing priorities.[3] At the time of this writing, the fate of the Oakland program hangs in the balance. When city budgets are tight, innovative public campaign finance programs designed to improve the responsiveness of elected officials often fall on the chopping block.

While Oakland is the only municipality outside of Seattle to pass a voucher program, organized movements are emerging in other cities to reform municipal elections. In Los Angeles, the City Council recently approved a motion to study the viability of a voucher program for local elections.[4] In San Diego, local reform groups are beginning to explore options for city elections, although no formal action has been taken by elected officials.[5] Reformers in Albuquerque, New Mexico, and Austin, Texas, have also pursued ballot propositions to establish voucher programs for eligible city offices, but both initiatives failed at the ballot box.[6]

The movements in these cities underscore the obstacles and opportunities for expanding the democracy voucher program beyond Seattle. To date, the municipalities that have undertaken organized efforts to introduce democracy dollars share several notable characteristics. Each of these cities is a medium-sized to large municipality ranging from a half-million people in Albuquerque to nearly 4 million in Los Angeles.[7] The cities that have pursued the program are all Democratic strongholds, reflecting the extent to which public campaign financing remains a partisan issue, even at the local level. But even in overwhelmingly Democratic cities, the movement to fund elections with public monies has sometimes been met with stiff resistance. Movement organizers face challenges in explaining the novel program to voters, consolidating voter support, and securing funding from elected officials. In fact, in most cities with new public campaign financing programs, elected leaders have chosen to adopt matching funds, like the ones we describe in Chapter 1, rather than voucher programs.

The obstacles to expansion are exacerbated by potential resistance from elected officials who may encounter increased electoral competition from public financing, too. In Chapter 2, we showed that the program has clearly chipped away at the incumbency advantage in Seattle, bringing more candidates and competition to local races. It has also introduced significant dynamism into the financing of local elections. Rather than relying on the same pool of donors each election cycle, candidates encounter a donor pool flush with new voucher users contributing to elections. While these changes are a gain for voters, they may be poorly received by entrenched incumbents with an existing set of contributors. Incumbents likely would prefer to avoid a primary challenge and an overhaul of their fundraising strategy necessitated by participation in a voucher program. Opposition to expanding the voucher program may thus come not only from tax-averse voters, but also from elected officials who prefer the status quo. In this way, the program could become a victim of its own success.

Several states have also pursued adopting the voucher program for funding statewide races. These efforts include bills introduced in the lower chambers of the Washington, Virginia, and New Hampshire state legislatures as well as a jettisoned provision in a larger package of democracy reforms passed in Minnesota.[8] Notably, the only successful statewide effort occurred in South Dakota. In the November 2016 elections, a majority of South Dakota voters approved an initiative that would have established a voucher program for state legislative and gubernatorial races. The initiative—which also included measures to reduce contribution limits, curb lobbying, and establish an ethics commission—generated a significant amount of controversy, attracting national attention as well as millions of dollars in spending by outside groups. The initiative was quickly repealed wholesale just two months later by a Republican-controlled legislature and governor.[9]

Building a National Program

While the Democracy Voucher program first gained traction at the local level, it was originally envisioned as a national program designed to transform the dynamics of federal elections. To date, only one significant attempt has been made to bring the democracy dollars program to national elections. The "For the People Act," or H.R. 1, was passed by the U.S. House of Representatives in 2021.[10] The bill contained a provision for a significant democracy dollars pilot program, called the "My Voice Voucher Pilot Program," which would be used in three states for their U.S. House elections. States would apply for participation in the program and then receive reimbursements for the cost of their vouchers. The pilot program stipulated that all registered voters receive five $5 vouchers or $25 in total to allocate in eligible races. Perhaps in anticipation of public resistance to paying for public campaign financing, the voucher pilot program in H.R. 1 was to be financed through a small surcharge on certain civil and criminal penalties.[11]

H.R. 1 was passed by a Democratic-led House of Representatives on a party-line vote in March 2021.[12] The bill quickly stalled, however, in the evenly divided Senate, where Democratic supporters struggled to convince more moderate members of their caucus or to attract bipartisan support.[13] The fate of H.R. 1 illustrates the hurdles to passage at the federal level. Support for public campaign finance measures—or any campaign finance reforms at all—has become an intensely partisan issue, with congressional Republicans unified in their opposition to holistic reform. Any democracy voucher program in particular is also unlikely to attract Republican support, given the program's demonstrated benefits for traditionally Democratic constituencies. The nation's two foundational campaign finance laws—the Federal Election Campaign Act (FECA) of 1974 and the Bipartisan Campaign Reform Act (BCRA) of 2002—were both passed with bipartisan support in Congress but would likely receive far less Republican buy-in today.[14]

In an era of deep partisan polarization among members of Congress, the path forward for any national campaign finance reform is unclear.[15] The stagnation of policymaking on this issue is especially striking given that large majorities of Americans—both Republicans and Democrats alike—express concern about the role of money in politics and even support new restrictions on political spending. When asked about spending in elections, most Americans recognize that large political donors have outsized influence and evince support for new laws that would reduce the role of money in American politics. This suspicion of the role of money in politics does not, however, necessarily translate into support for public campaign financing, especially if funding such a program would require new or higher taxes. In the end, it is doubtful that Republican voters would support any public campaign finance program, given the entrenched resistance of the party to government spending.

The Unfinished Business of Democracy Reform

As the program in Seattle hurtles toward its ten-year anniversary, there remain many unanswered questions about the future of campaign finance reform. Is Seattle's success the beginning of a far-reaching movement to reform the way elections are financed? Will the program gain momentum toward adoption in other cities, and can this momentum inspire state and federal reforms? Does the Democracy Voucher program foretell a new model of funding campaigns, or will Seattle ultimately remain as a one-time experiment in democracy reform?

The experience of Seattle over the last decade underscores many of the core obstacles to widespread adoption. The resistance of tax-averse voters and the persistence of partisan polarization will continue to shape the possibilities for expansion. As city leaders struggle with a host of social challenges, including a crisis of housing affordability and emergent threats to public safety, they must find the resources to devote to these immediate urban issues. Whether or not democracy reforms aimed at improving electoral fairness will emerge as a top concern of voters and policymakers, especially during periods of budget austerity, remains to be seen.

At the same time, the expansion of the program beyond Seattle may fall victim to its own success. As incumbents come to understand the example of Seattle, they may fear the disruptions to the status quo inherent in a voucher program. Quite often, it is incumbent politicians, rather than their challengers, who benefit from long lists of donors. When they do support public financing of local elections, policymakers may have reason to prefer alternative forms, such as matching funds, that are less disruptive to existing patterns of fundraising. They may also object to the rise of outside spending that appears to accompany publicly financed campaigns. These are existential questions about the future of these programs—questions made more pressing by the number of localities considering adoption. Does outside spending—even if driven by increased electoral competition—undermine the significant gains the program has made vis-à-vis participation and representation?

The future of the program may also importantly hinge on its success in delivering more equitable policy outcomes for all residents. The program has laid the groundwork for a more equal city, but whether it can deliver a real difference in the distribution of city services remains an open question. Policy outcomes can be both slow to appear and hard to measure, raising the possibility that the program's most significant impacts will go undetected and unappreciated by voters. So far, the evidence suggests that the program is increasing descriptive representation in city elections and among elected officials. While those changes are a good first step, maintaining the program in Seattle and building momentum outside the city will require evidence linking these democracy reforms to a fairer, more inclusive urban polity.

Notes

INTRODUCTION

    1. Gene Balk, "The Seattle Area Has Gotten Even More Liberal—Here's Why," *Seattle Times*, February 24, 2020, available at https://www.seattletimes.com/seattle-news/data/blue-bump-democratic-supporters-now-make-up-majority-of-adults-in-snohomish-and-king-counties/.

    2. Gene Balk, "Where King County Ranks amid the 'Bluest' Counties in the Nation," *Seattle Times*, November 10, 2022, available at https://www.seattletimes.com/seattle-news/data/king-county-is-not-the-bluest-big-u-s-county-but-were-close/.

    3. U.S. Census Bureau, "DP1: Profile of General Demographic Characteristics: 2000," 2000, available at https://data.census.gov/table?g=160XX00US5363000&y=2000&tid=DECENNIALDPSF42000.DP1; U.S. Census Bureau, "U.S. Census Bureau QuickFacts: Seattle City, Washington," 2022, https://www.census.gov/quickfacts/fact/table/seattlecitywashington/PST045222.

    4. Richard Florida, *The New Urban Crisis: How Our Cities Are Increasing Inequality, Deepening Segregation, and Failing the Middle Class—and What We Can Do About It*, 1st ed. (New York: Basic Books, 2017).

    5. In 2010, Seattle's unadjusted median income was $60,212.

    6. South Lake Union Chamber of Commerce, "Construction & Development," *South Lake Union Chamber of Commerce* (blog), 2023, available at https://www.sluchamber.org/construction-development/.

    7. Katharine Swindells, "Income in US Cities Is Most Unevenly Distributed in a Decade," *City Monitor* (blog), December 22, 2022, available at https://citymonitor.ai/community/neighbourhoods/us-income-inequality-cities-revealed.

    8. Swindells, "Income in US Cities."

    9. Swindells, "Income in US Cities."

10. U.S. Census Bureau, "S1701: Poverty Status in the Past 12 Months," 2021, available at https://data.census.gov/table?t=Poverty&g=160XX00US5363000&tid=ACSST1Y2021 .S1701.

11. U.S. Census Bureau, "DP05: ACS Demographic and Housing Estimates," 2021, available at https://data.census.gov/table?g=160XX00US5363000.

12. U.S. Census Bureau, "S1701: Poverty Status in the Past 12 Months."

13. Gregg Colburn and Clayton Page Aldern, *Homelessness Is a Housing Problem: How Structural Factors Explain U.S. Patterns* (Berkeley: University of California Press, 2022).

14. "City of Seattle, 'Charter Amendment 19,'" Office of the City Clerk, 2013, https:// clerk.seattle.gov/~CFs/CF_313380.pdf.

15. Ann O'M. Bowman, *Reinventing the Austin City Council*, Political Lessons from American Cities (Philadelphia: Temple University Press, 2020).

16. King County Board of Elections, "Election Results, November 03, 2020," 2020, available at https://aqua.kingcounty.gov/elections/2020/nov-general/results.pdf.

17. King County Board of Elections, "Election Results, November 02, 2021," 2021, available at https://aqua.kingcounty.gov/elections/2021/nov-general/results.pdf.

18. Portland State University, "Who Votes for Mayor?" 2016, available at http://who votesformayor.org/compare.

19. King County Board of Elections, "Election Results, November 05, 2019," 2019, available at https://aqua.kingcounty.gov/elections/2019/nov-general/results.pdf.

20. Sidney Verba, Kay Lehman Schlozman, and Henry E. Brady, *Voice and Equality: Civic Voluntarism in American Politics* (Cambridge, MA: Harvard University Press, 1995).

21. Jennifer Heerwig and Brian J. McCabe, "High-Dollar Donors and Donor-Rich Neighborhoods: Representational Distortion in Financing a Municipal Election in Seattle," *Urban Affairs Review* 55, no. 4 (July 2019): 1070–1099, available at https://doi.org /10.1177/1078087417728378.

22. Heerwig and McCabe, "High-Dollar Donors and Donor-Rich Neighborhoods."

23. Associated Press, "Socialist Sworn In as Seattle City Council Member," *USA Today,* January 6, 2014, available at https://www.usatoday.com/story/news/nation/2014/01/06 /socialist-seattle-city-council/4349923/.

24. Casey Martin, "Looking Back at Seattle's CHOP, One Year Later," KUOW, June 7, 2021, available at https://www.kuow.org/stories/looking-back-at-seattle-s-chop-one -year-later.

25. Joseph Parilla and Glencora Haskins, "Metro Monitor 2023," Brookings, 2023, available at https://www.brookings.edu/articles/metro-monitor-2023/.

26. Meghan Joy and Ronald K. Vogel, "Beyond Neoliberalism: A Policy Agenda for a Progressive City," *Urban Affairs Review* 57, no. 5 (September 2021): 1372–1409, available at https://doi.org/10.1177/1078087420984241.

27. Seattle Municipal Archives, "Ballot Initiatives—CityArchives," 2023, available at https://www.seattle.gov/cityarchives/seattle-facts/ballot-initiatives.

28. Joy and Vogel, "Beyond Neoliberalism."

29. Steven Greenhouse, "With Day of Protests, Fast-Food Workers Seek More Pay," *New York Times,* November 30, 2012, New York sec., available at https://www.nytimes .com/2012/11/30/nyregion/fast-food-workers-in-new-york-city-rally-for-higher-wages.html.

30. Seattle Office of Labor Standards, "App-Based Worker Paid Sick and Safe Time Ordinance," 2023, available at https://www.seattle.gov/laborstandards/ordinances/app -based-worker-paid-sick-and-safe-time-ordinance#.

31. Seattle Office of Labor Standards, "Domestic Workers," 2023, available at https://www.seattle.gov/laborstandards/ordinances/domestic-workers#:~:text=Seattle%20is%20the%20first%20city,a%20Domestic%20Workers%20Standards%20Board.

32. Eilis O'Neill, "Landlords Must Rent First-Come, First-Served," KUOW, November 15, 2019, available at https://www.kuow.org/stories/landlords-must-rent-first-come-first-served.

33. Seattle Municipal Archives, "2015–2019 Ballot Initiatives," 2023, available at https://www.seattle.gov/cityarchives/seattle-facts/ballot-initiatives#20152019ballotinitiatives.

34. Jennifer A. Heerwig, "Money in the Middle: Contribution Strategies among Affluent Donors to Federal Elections, 1980–2008," *American Journal of Sociology* 123, no. 4 (January 2018): 1004–1063, available at https://doi.org/10.1086/694888.

CHAPTER 1

1. Center for Responsive Politics, "Most Expensive Ever: 2020 Election Cost $14.4 Billion," OpenSecrets News, February 11, 2021, available at https://www.opensecrets.org/news/2021/02/2020-cycle-cost-14p4-billion-doubling-16/.

2. Campaign Finance Institute, "The Cost of Winning an Election, 1986–2018," 2022, available at http://www.cfinst.org/pdf/federal/HistoricalTables/pdf/CFI_Federal-CF_18_Table2-01.pdf.

3. Paul S. Herrnson, Costas Panagopoulos, and Kendall L. Bailey, *Congressional Elections: Campaigning at Home and in Washington*, 8th ed. (Thousand Oaks, CA: SAGE/CQ Press, 2020).

4. Peter L. Francia and Paul S. Herrnson, "The Impact of Public Finance Laws on Fundraising in State Legislative Elections," *American Politics Research* 31, no. 5 (September 2003): 520–539, available at https://doi.org/10.1177/1532673X03256784.

5. Adam Bonica, "Professional Networks, Early Fundraising, and Electoral Success," *Election Law Journal: Rules, Politics, and Policy* 16, no. 1 (2017): 153–171, available at https://doi.org/10.1089/elj.2016.0413.

6. OpenSecrets, "Elections Overview, 2020," OpenSecrets News, 2023, available at https://www.opensecrets.org/elections-overview?cycle=2020&display=T&type=A.

7. Herrnson, Panagopoulos, and Bailey, *Congressional Elections*.

8. Campaign Finance Institute, "Table 2-8: House Receipts from Individuals, PACs, and Others, All General Election Candidates, 1999–2018," 2018, available at http://www.cfinst.org/pdf/federal/HistoricalTables/pdf/CFI_Federal-CF_18_Table2-08.pdf.

9. Kay Lehman Schlozman, Sidney Verba, and Henry E. Brady, *The Unheavenly Chorus: Unequal Political Voice and the Broken Promise of American Democracy* (Princeton, NJ: Princeton University Press, 2012), available at https://doi.org/10.1515/9781400841912.

10. Center for Responsive Politics, "Donor Demographics," OpenSecrets News, 2022, available at https://www.opensecrets.org/elections-overview/donor-demographics?cycle=2018&display=A.

11. Verba, Schlozman, and Brady, *Voice and Equality*; Daniel Laurison, "Social Class and Political Engagement in the United States," *Sociology Compass* 10, no. 8 (2016): 684–697.

12. Peter Francia et al., *The Financiers of Congressional Elections: Investors, Ideologues, and Intimates* (New York: Columbia University Press, 2003), available at https://doi.org/10.7312/fran11618.

13. Jacob M. Grumbach and Alexander Sahn, "Race and Representation in Campaign Finance," *American Political Science Review* 114, no. 1 (February 2020): 206–221, available at https://doi.org/10.1017/S0003055419000637.

14. Dan Clawson, Alan Neustadtl, and Mark Weller, *Dollars and Votes: How Business Campaign Contributions Subvert Democracy* (Philadelphia: Temple University Press, 1998).

15. Joshua L. Kalla and David E. Broockman, "Campaign Contributions Facilitate Access to Congressional Officials: A Randomized Field Experiment," *American Journal of Political Science* 60, no. 3 (July 2016): 545–558, available at https://doi.org/10.1111/ajps.12180.

16. Thomas Stratmann, "Some Talk: Money in Politics. A (Partial) Review of the Literature," *Public Choice* 124, nos. 1–2 (July 2005): 135–156, available at https://doi.org/10.1007/s11127-005-4750-3; Martin Gilens and Benjamin I. Page, "Testing Theories of American Politics: Elites, Interest Groups, and Average Citizens," *Perspectives on Politics* 12, no. 3 (September 2014): 564–581, available at https://doi.org/10.1017/S1537592714001595; Amy Melissa McKay, "Fundraising for Favors? Linking Lobbyist-Hosted Fundraisers to Legislative Benefits," *Political Research Quarterly* 71, no. 4 (December 2018): 869–880, available at https://doi.org/10.1177/1065912918771745; Theda Skocpol and Alexander Hertel-Fernandez, "The Koch Network and Republican Party Extremism," *Perspectives on Politics* 14, no. 3 (September 2016): 681–699, available at https://doi.org/10.1017/S1537592716001122; Larry M. Bartels, *Unequal Democracy: The Political Economy of the New Gilded Age*, 2d ed. (Princeton, NJ: Princeton University Press, 2018); Benjamin I. Page, Larry M. Bartels, and Jason Seawright, "Democracy and the Policy Preferences of Wealthy Americans," *Perspectives on Politics* 11, no. 1 (March 2013): 51–73, available at https://doi.org/10.1017/S153759271200360X.

17. Martin Gilens, *Affluence and Influence: Economic Inequality and Political Power in America* (Princeton, NJ: Princeton University Press, 2012), available at https://doi.org/10.1515/9781400844821; Bartels, *Unequal Democracy*.

18. U.S. Census Bureau, "Congressional Apportionment," November 2011, available at https://www.census.gov/prod/cen2010/briefs/c2010br-08.pdf.

19. Ann O'M. Bowman and Richard C. Kearney, *State and Local Government* (Boston: Cengage Learning, 2016).

20. Zoltan L. Hajnal and Paul G. Lewis, "Municipal Institutions and Voter Turnout in Local Elections," *Urban Affairs Review* 38, no. 5 (May 1, 2003): 645–668, available at https://doi.org/10.1177/1078087403038005002.

21. King County Board of Elections, "Election Results, November 02, 2021."

22. Clarence Nathan Stone, *Regime Politics: Governing Atlanta, 1946–1988* (Lawrence: University Press of Kansas, 1989); Clarence N. Stone, "Urban Regimes and the Capacity to Govern: A Political Economy Approach," *Journal of Urban Affairs* 15, no. 1 (March 1993): 1–28, available at https://doi.org/10.1111/j.1467-9906.1993.tb00300.x; Brian E. Adams, "Campaign Finance in Local Elections: Buying the Grassroots," in *Campaign Finance in Local Elections* (Boulder, CO: Lynne Rienner Publishers, 2022), available at https://doi.org/10.1515/9781626371705; Brian E. Adams, "Suburban Money in Central City Elections: The Geographic Distribution of Campaign Contributions," *Urban Affairs Review* 42, no. 2 (November 2006): 267–280, available at https://doi.org/10.1177/1078087406292699; Brian E. Adams, "Fundraising Coalitions in Open Seat Mayoral Elections," *Journal of Urban Affairs* 29, no. 5 (December 2007): 481–499, available at https://doi.org/10.1111/j.1467-9906.2007.00361.x; Timothy B. Krebs,

"Urban Interests and Campaign Contributions: Evidence from Los Angeles," *Journal of Urban Affairs* 27, no. 2 (June 2005): 165–176, available at https://doi.org/10.1111/j.0735 -2166.2005.00230.x; Timothy B. Krebs and John P. Pelissero, "Fund-Raising Coalitions in Mayoral Campaigns," *Urban Affairs Review* 37, no. 1 (September 2001): 67–84, available at https://doi.org/10.1177/10780870122185190; Arnold Fleischmann and Lana Stein, "Campaign Contributions in Local Elections," *Political Research Quarterly* 51, no. 3 (September 1998): 673–689, available at https://doi.org/10.1177/106591299805100306.

23. Brian F. Schaffner, Jesse H. Rhodes, and Raymond J. La Raja, *Hometown Inequality: Race, Class, and Representation in American Local Politics* (Cambridge: Cambridge University Press, 2020); J. Eric Oliver, Shang E. Ha, and Zachary Callen, *Local Elections and the Politics of Small-Scale Democracy* (Princeton, NJ: Princeton University Press, 2012), available at https://doi.org/10.1515/9781400842544.

24. Schaffner, Rhodes, and La Raja, *Hometown Inequality*.

25. Zoltan Hajnal and Jessica Trounstine, "Identifying and Understanding Perceived Inequities in Local Politics," *Political Research Quarterly* 67, no. 1 (March 2014): 56–70, available at https://doi.org/10.1177/1065912913486728; Zoltan Hajnal and Jessica Trounstine, "Where Turnout Matters: The Consequences of Uneven Turnout in City Politics," *Journal of Politics* 67, no. 2 (May 2005): 515–535, available at https://doi.org/10.1111 /j.1468-2508.2005.00327.x; Katherine Levine Einstein, Maxwell Palmer, and David M. Glick, "Who Participates in Local Government? Evidence from Meeting Minutes," *Perspectives on Politics* 17, no. 1 (March 2019): 28–46, available at https://doi.org/10.1017 /S153759271800213X.

26. Federal Election Commission, "Contribution Limits," FEC.gov, 2022, available at https://www.fec.gov/help-candidates-and-committees/candidate-taking-receipts /contribution-limits/.

27. So-called aggregate limits on campaign contributions were struck down by the U.S. Supreme Court in *McCutcheon v. FEC* in 2014.

28. Jennifer Heerwig and Katherine Shaw, "Through a Glass, Darkly: The Rhetoric and Reality of Campaign Finance Disclosure," *Georgetown Law Journal* 102 (2014): 1443.

29. *Buckley v. Valeo*, 424 U.S. 1 (1976).

30. Richard Briffault, "Home Rule and Local Political Innovation," *Journal of Law & Politics* 22 (2006): 1.

31. Although there is still a federal public financing program in place for presidential campaigns, the program has been largely abandoned by modern candidates. We discuss this in further detail in Chapter 3.

32. Francia and Herrnson, "The Impact of Public Finance Laws"; Michael J. Malbin and Michael Parrott, "Small Donor Empowerment Depends on the Details: Comparing Matching Fund Programs in New York and Los Angeles," *The Forum* 15, no. 2 (July 2017): 219–250, available at https://doi.org/10.1515/for-2017-0015; Michael J. Malbin, Peter W. Brusoe, and Brendan Glavin, "Small Donors, Big Democracy: New York City's Matching Funds as a Model for the Nation and States," *Election Law Journal: Rules, Politics, and Policy* 11, no. 1 (March 2012): 3–20, available at https://doi.org/10.1089 /elj.2010.0099; Michael J. Malbin, "Citizen Funding for Elections: What Do We Know? What Are the Effects? What Are the Options?" (Washington, DC: Campaign Finance Institute, 2015), available at http://www.cfinst.org/pdf/books-reports/CFI_Citizen FundingforElections.pdf.

33. Michael G. Miller, *Subsidizing Democracy: How Public Funding Changes Elections and How It Can Work in the Future* (Ithaca, NY: Cornell University Press, 2013).

34. The size of a qualifying candidate's lump-sum grant in the general election depends on the office sought, the level of opposition the candidate faces, when the candidate applies for public funds, and whether the candidate has used any personal funds to finance their campaign. See Connecticut State Elections Enforcement Commission, "Grant Application and Amounts," 2022, available at https://seec.ct.gov/Portal/CEP /Grants.

35. City Clerk City of Austin, "Austin Fair Campaigns," Pub. L. No. 20080925-079, Austin City Code (2008), available at https://services.austintexas.gov/edims/document. cfm%3Fid%3D121599; Demos, "Public Funding for Electoral Campaigns: How 27 States, Counties and Municipalities Empower Small Donors and Curb the Power of Big Money in Politics" (New York: Demos, 2017), available at https://www.demos.org/sites/default /files/publications/Public_Financing_Factsheet_FA%5B5%5D.pdf; Dan Way, "Chapel Hill Shuts Down Matching Funds for Local Elections," *Carolina Journal*, September 15, 2011, available at https://www.carolinajournal.com/chapel-hill-shuts-down-matching -funds-for-local-elections/.

36. Miller, *Subsidizing Democracy*.

37. Demos, "Public Funding for Electoral Campaigns"; Brian McCabe and Kenan Dogan, "The Fair Elections Program Is Reshaping the Campaign Finance System in DC, Increasing Candidate and New Donor Participation," *McCourt School of Public Policy* (blog), September 19, 2021, available at https://mccourt.georgetown.edu/news/dc-fair -elections-program/.

38. New York City Campaign Finance Board, "Limits & Thresholds," 2021, available at https://www.nyccfb.info/candidate-services/limits-thresholds/2021/.

39. New York City Campaign Finance Board, "Limits & Thresholds."

40. Malbin and Parrott, "Small Donor Empowerment Depends on the Details."

41. Malbin and Parrott, "Small Donor Empowerment Depends on the Details."

42. Spencer Overton, "The Participation Interest," *Georgetown Law Journal* 100 (2012): 1259.

43. An earlier proposal for a voucher-like system traces back to Senator Lee Metcalf in 1967. Adamany and Agree further developed the idea. See David Adamany and George Agree, *Political Money: A Strategy for Campaign Financing in America* (Baltimore: Johns Hopkins University Press, 1975).

44. Bruce Ackerman, "Crediting the Voters: A New Beginning for Campaign Finance," *American Prospect*, April 1, 1993, available at https://prospect.org/api/content/0b1bf27b -4790-5ff6-9e59-4700ac2aa633/.

45. Ackerman, "Crediting the Voters."

46. Bruce Ackerman and Ian Ayres, *Voting with Dollars: A New Paradigm for Campaign Finance* (New Haven, CT: Yale University Press, 2002).

47. Ackerman and Ayres, *Voting with Dollars*; David A. Strauss, "What's the Problem? Ackerman and Ayres on Campaign Finance Reform," *California Law Review* 91, no. 3 (May 2003): 723, available at https://doi.org/10.2307/3481375.

48. Strauss, "What's the Problem?" 724.

49. Lawrence Lessig, *Republic, Lost: How Money Corrupts Congress—and a Plan to Stop It* (New York: Hachette, 2012); Lawrence Lessig, "More Money Can Beat Big Money," *New York Times*, November 17, 2011, available at https://www.nytimes.com/2011/11/17 /opinion/in-campaign-financing-more-money-can-beat-big-money.html.

50. Lessig, *Republic, Lost*.

51. This section is based on interviews with local leaders, organizers, and reformers who were involved with the Honest Elections Seattle campaign.

52. Herbert E. Alexander and Michael C. Walker, "Public Financing of Local Elections: A Data Book on Public Funding in Four Cities and Two Counties" (Los Angeles: University of Southern California/Citizens' Research Foundation, 1990).

53. Alexander and Walker, "Public Financing of Local Elections."

54. "Public funds, whether derived through taxes, fees, penalties, or any other sources, shall not be used to finance political campaigns for state or local office." See the Revised Code of Washington, 42.17.128, available at https://apps.leg.wa.gov/rcw/dispo .aspx?cite=42.17.128.

55. "Public funds, whether derived through taxes, fees, penalties, or any other sources, shall not be used to finance political campaigns for state or school district office. A county, city, town, or district that establishes a program to publicly finance local political campaigns may only use funds derived from local sources to fund the program. A local government must submit any proposal for public financing of local political campaigns to voters for their adoption and approval or rejection." See the Revised Code of Washington, 42.17A.550, available at https://apps.leg.wa.gov/rcw/default.aspx?cite=42.17A.550.

56. That year, the voters also considered Charter Amendment #19 to reform the structure of the City Council.

57. According to public records, Fair Elections Seattle's expenditures were primarily used to finance political consultants and legal fees and pay for internal polling for the campaign.

58. Liz Dupee and Alissa Haslam, "The Honest Elections Seattle Story" (unpublished working paper, n.d.).

59. Tim Burgess, "Public Campaign Finance: Right Idea, Wrong Time," Seattle Forward, 2014, available at https://www.timburgess.com/2014/06/public-campaign-finance -right-idea-wrong-time.html.

60. Doug McAdam, *Political Process and the Development of Black Insurgency, 1930–1970* (Chicago: University of Chicago Press, 1999); David S. Meyer and Suzanne Staggenborg, "Movements, Countermovements, and the Structure of Political Opportunity," *American Journal of Sociology* 101, no. 6 (May 1996): 1628–1660, available at https://doi .org/10.1086/230869.

61. The focus group was paid for by the coalition and convened by Lake Research Partners.

62. Daniel Beekman, "Seattle Initiative Drive Seeks Public Campaign Financing, Reform," *Seattle Times*, April 3, 2015, available at https://www.seattletimes.com/seattle -news/politics/seattle-initiative-drive-seeks-public-campaign-financing-reform/.

63. Beekman, "Seattle Initiative Drive."

64. Honest Elections Seattle, "What Is Initiative 122?" 2015, available at https:// web.archive.org/web/20150427235155/http://honestelectionsseattle.org/what-is-initia tive-122/.

65. Daniel Beekman, "Seattle's Richest, Whitest Areas Dominate Campaign Giving, Say Reform Backers," *Seattle Times*, July 21, 2015, available at https://www.seattletimes .com/seattle-news/politics/seattles-richest-whitest-sway-campaign-giving-say-reform -backers/; Alan Durning, "Who Funds Seattle's Political Candidates?" (Seattle: Sightline Institute, July 2015), available at https://www.sightline.org/2015/07/22/who-funds -seattles-political-candidates/.

66. Honest Elections Seattle, "What Is Initiative 122?"

67. Honest Elections Seattle, "What Is Initiative 122?"

68. Remarkably, large local employers such as Amazon, Starbucks, and Boeing did not mobilize to oppose the reform effort. Instead, these corporations were later drawn

into local politics over a proposed City Council measure to raise taxes on large local employers in the 2019 election.

69. Daniel Beekman, "I-122: Big Money Helping Wage Anti-Big-Money Campaign," *Seattle Times*, October 26, 2015, Local Politics sec., available at https://www.seattletimes. com/seattle-news/politics/i-122-big-money-helping-wage-anti-big-money-campaign/; Bob Young, "'Democracy Vouchers' Win in Seattle; First in Country," *Seattle Times*, November 3, 2015, available at https://www.seattletimes.com/seattle-news/politics /democracy-vouchers/.

70. Beekman, "I-122."

71. Young, "'Democracy Vouchers' Win in Seattle; First in Country."

72. Young, "'Democracy Vouchers' Win in Seattle; First in Country."

73. Julia Cagé, *The Price of Democracy: How Money Shapes Politics and What to Do about It* (Cambridge, MA: Harvard University Press, 2020).

74. Connecticut State Elections Enforcement Commission, "Grant Application and Amounts."

CHAPTER 2

1. Overton, "The Participation Interest."

2. Grumbach and Sahn, "Race and Representation in Campaign Finance."

3. Schaffner, Rhodes, and La Raja, *Hometown Inequality*, 13.

4. Zoltan L. Hajnal, *America's Uneven Democracy: Race, Turnout, and Representation in City Politics* (Cambridge: Cambridge University Press, 2009).

5. Participating mayoral candidates had the same $550 contribution limit as nonparticipating mayoral candidates in 2021. However, the $550 contribution limit for participating mayoral candidates included a $50 maximum voucher donation. In other words, a participating mayoral candidate could receive up to $550 in cash or $500 in cash plus $50 in vouchers.

6. After being validated by the Seattle Ethics and Elections Commission (SEEC), voucher funds are formally redeemed and released to qualified candidates. Candidates receive redemption checks from the SEEC approximately twice per month until the candidate has reached the applicable voucher maximum. Once a candidate receives the maximum in vouchers, the candidate's campaign can no longer receive any voucher money even if it is assigned to them. This means that during every cycle there are vouchers that have been assigned to qualified candidates but cannot be redeemed under program rules. This feature of the program—that assigned vouchers cannot be redeemed by candidates after the maximum is reached—has met with some criticism for possibly discouraging voters from supporting a popular or strong candidate. We return to this issue in the next chapter.

7. Jeffrey Kraus, "Campaign Finance Reform Reconsidered: New York City's Public Finance Program at Twenty," in *Public Financing in American Elections*, ed. Costas Panagopoulos (Philadelphia: Temple University Press, 2011), available at http://www .jstor.org/stable/j.cttl4btbh8.9; Miller, *Subsidizing Democracy.*

8. Under the program's rules, Seattle residents do not have to be registered to vote to participate in the program. Any Seattle resident may apply to receive democracy vouchers if they are eighteen years of age or older, a Seattle resident, and a U.S. national or permanent resident. Although the program is technically open to nonvoters, the number of permanent residents who apply to receive vouchers has been small.

9. Paper vouchers assigned to local candidates must be signed by the voter before being returned. These signatures are then validated by the King County Board of Elections using signatures on record for voter registrations. Voters assigning vouchers through the online portal must validate their identity by providing their birthdate and last four digits of their social security number. Whether returned by paper or online, each voucher is reviewed by staff before being formally allocated to a participating candidate's campaign.

10. Authors' analysis of SEEC data.

11. Berk Consulting, "Seattle Democracy Voucher Program Evaluation," 2018, available at https://www.seattle.gov/documents/Departments/EthicsElections/Democra cyVoucher/Biennial%20Reports/DVP%20Evaluation%20Final%20Report%20April% 2025%202018.pdf; Berk Consulting, "2019 Election Cycle Evaluation" (Seattle, WA: Berk Consulting, 2020), available at https://www.seattle.gov/documents/Departments/Ethics Elections/DemocracyVoucher/Biennial%20Reports/Final%20DVP%20Evaluation%20 Report%20July23_2020.pdf.

12. We include all residents who assigned a voucher, regardless of whether the voucher was ultimately redeemed, to emphasize participation rather than adherence to program rules.

13. Alan Griffith and Thomas Noonen, "The Effects of Public Campaign Funding: Evidence from Seattle's Democracy Voucher Program," *Journal of Public Economics* 211 (July 2022): 104676, available at https://doi.org/10.1016/j.jpubeco.2022.104676.

14. For evidence of the program's effects on voter participation, see also Sarah Papich, "Do Democracy Vouchers Help Democracy?" *Contemporary Economic Policy* 42, no. 1 (2024): 4–24, available at https://doi.org/10.1111/coep.12625.

15. Francia et al., "The Financiers of Congressional Elections."

16. Clawson, Neustadtl, and Weller, *Dollars and Votes*.

17. Disclosure records contain lists of individual donations but do not aggregate donations originating from the same individual. We used a probabilistic matching algorithm—available in the "reclin2\" package in R—to link cash donation records from unique individuals across election cycles. Our panel contains a donor identification number for everyone who donated in Seattle elections between 2013 and 2021.

18. Jennifer Heerwig and Brian J. McCabe, "Broadening Donor Participation in Local Elections: Results from the Seattle Democracy Voucher Program in 2021" (Washington, DC: McCourt School of Public Policy, Georgetown University, 2022), available at https:// mccourt.georgetown.edu/wp-content/uploads/2022/08/Broadening-Donor-Participa tion-in-Local-Elections_Report_2022.pdf.

19. Our proprietary voter file data comes from TargetSmart. TargetSmart data has been used in a variety of academic studies of political behavior. We use the TargetSmart voter files for 2013, 2015, 2017, 2019, and 2021 to describe the sociodemographic characteristics of voters, donors, and voucher users. We rely on TargetSmart's age variable (derived from voter registration records), race (a modeled variable from proprietary consumer and voter data), and income (modeled from consumer data). As we note, however, some caution is warranted in interpreting the results of the income measure. For examples of other studies that use TargetSmart data, see Sharad Goel et al., "One Person, One Vote: Estimating the Prevalence of Double Voting in U.S. Presidential Elections," *American Political Science Review* 114, no. 2 (May 2020): 456–469, available at https://doi.org/10.1017/S000305541900087X; Shanto Iyengar, Tobias Konitzer, and Kent Tedin, "The Home as a Political Fortress: Family Agreement in an Era of Polar-

ization," *Journal of Politics* 80, no. 4 (October 2018): 1326–1338, available at https://doi
.org/10.1086/698929.

20. Verba, Schlozman, and Brady, *Voice and Equality*, 189–196.

21. Verba, Schlozman, and Brady, *Voice and Equality*, 231–239; Schlozman, Verba, and Brady, *Unheavenly Chorus*, 215–219.

22. The household income measure available in the voter file is a modeled variable derived from commercial marketing data sources. As such, the results for this measure should be interpreted with some caution.

23. Jacob M. Grumbach and Charlotte Hill, "Rock the Registration: Same Day Registration Increases Turnout of Young Voters," *Journal of Politics* 84, no. 1 (January 2022): 405–417, available at https://doi.org/10.1086/714776.

24. To simplify our analyses, we compare voucher users to voters in the concurrent year's local general elections. This comparison may understate representational disparities relative to registered voters or to the full Seattle population. Further, we exclude so-called "qualifying donors" in our cash donor category because qualifying donors are, arguably, a special category of donors that resulted from the Democracy Voucher program itself. The cash donor category includes all cash donors who donated—regardless of the size of their donation—outside the qualification period.

25. Verba, Schlozman, and Brady, *Voice and Equality*, 23–24.

26. Griffith and Noonen, "Effects of Public Campaign Funding."

27. Bonica, "Professional Networks, Early Fundraising, and Electoral Success."

28. Herrnson, Panagopoulos, and Bailey, *Congressional Elections*.

29. Mirya R. Holman, "Women in Local Government: What We Know and Where We Go from Here," *State & Local Government Review* 49, no. 4 (2017): 285–296; Patricia A. Kirkland, "Representation in American Cities: Who Runs for Mayor and Who Wins?" *Urban Affairs Review* 58, no. 3 (May 2022): 635–670, available at https://doi .org/10.1177/10780874211021688; Schaffner, Rhodes, and La Raja, *Hometown Inequality*, 99.

30. Lonna Rae Atkeson and Nancy Carrillo, "More Is Better: The Influence of Collective Female Descriptive Representation on External Efficacy," *Politics & Gender* 3, no. 1 (March 2007): 79–101, available at https://doi.org/10.1017/S1743923X0707002X; Andy Baker and Corey Cook, "Representing Black Interests and Promoting Black Culture: The Importance of African American Descriptive Representation in the U.S. House," *Du Bois Review: Social Science Research on Race* 2, no. 2 (September 2005): 227–246, available at https://doi.org/10.1017/S1742058X05050162; Donald P. Haider-Markel, "Representation and Backlash: The Positive and Negative Influence of Descriptive Representation," *Legislative Studies Quarterly* 32, no. 1 (2007): 107–133, available at https:// doi.org/10.3162/036298007X202001; Matthew Hayes and Matthew V. Hibbing, "The Symbolic Benefits of Descriptive and Substantive Representation," *Political Behavior* 39, no. 1 (March 2017): 31–50, available at https://doi.org/10.1007/s11109-016-9345-9; Beth Reingold and Jessica Harrell, "The Impact of Descriptive Representation on Women's Political Engagement: Does Party Matter?" *Political Research Quarterly* 63, no. 2 (June 2010): 280–294, available at https://doi.org/10.1177/1065912908330346; Katherine Tate, "The Political Representation of Blacks in Congress: Does Race Matter?" *Legislative Studies Quarterly* 26, no. 4 (2001): 623–638, available at https://doi.org/10.2307/440272; Stacy G. Ulbig, "Gendering Municipal Government: Female Descriptive Representation and Feelings of Political Trust," *Social Science Quarterly* 88, no. 5 (2007): 1106–1123, available at https://doi.org/10.1111/j.1540-6237.2007.00494.x.

31. Schaffner, Rhodes, and La Raja, *Hometown Inequality*, 106.

32. Authors' calculation using SEEC data. Candidate information can be accessed at http://web6.seattle.gov/ethics/elections/campaigns.aspx.

33. Daniel Beekman, "Seattle Candidates Again Vie for 'Democracy Vouchers' as They Pivot to November Election," *Seattle Times*, September 6, 2021, available at https://www.seattletimes.com/seattle-news/politics/seattle-candidates-again-vie-for-democracy-vouchers-as-they-pivot-to-november-election/; Rich Smith, "Kshama Sawant Says She Won't Use Democracy Vouchers. Why Not?" The Stranger, 2019, available at https://www.thestranger.com/news/2019/01/24/38277781/kshama-sawant-says-she-wont-use-democracy-vouchers-why-not.

34. Griffith and Noonen, "Effects of Public Campaign Funding."

35. Griffith and Noonen, "Effects of Public Campaign Funding."

36. This section draws on original interviews we conducted with City Council candidates between March 2022 and March 2023.

37. Berk Consulting, "Seattle Democracy Voucher Program Evaluation"; Berk Consulting, "2019 Election Cycle Evaluation."

38. Gary C. Jacobson and Jamie L. Carson, *The Politics of Congressional Elections* (Lanham, MD: Rowman & Littlefield, 2019); Adams, "Campaign Finance in Local Elections."

39. Griffith and Noonen, "Effects of Public Campaign Funding," 10.

40. Griffith and Noonen, "Effects of Public Campaign Funding."

41. Candidates were linked to the TargetSmart voter file using last and first names. In the case of duplicate matches, records were manually inspected to identify the candidate using publicly available identifying information such as address, age, and/or occupation.

42. Schaffner, Rhodes, and La Raja, *Hometown Inequality*, 99.

43. Schaffner, Rhodes, and La Raja, *Hometown Inequality*.

44. Matthew Powers, Sandra Vera Zambrano, and Olivier Baisnée, "The News Crisis Compared: The Impact of the Journalism Crisis on Local News Ecosystems in Toulouse (France) and Seattle (US)," in *Local Journalism: The Decline of Newspapers and the Rise of Digital Media*, ed. Rasmus Kleis Nielsen, 1st ed. (London: I. B. Tauris, 2015); Rasmus Kleis Nielsen, "Local Newspapers as Keystone Media: The Increased Importance of Diminished Newspapers for Local Political Information Environments," in Nielsen, *Local Journalism*.

CHAPTER 3

1. This calculation assumes that there are four qualified candidates in each of seven districts, for a total of twenty-one candidates in the primary election. Given the primary spending cap of $93,750 for districted council races, this would translate into 21 × $93,750 = $1,968,750. Of those twenty-one candidates, two from each district would advance to the general election, for a total of fourteen candidates. Given the general spending cap of $93,750, this would translate into 14 × $93,750 = $1,312,500. Total voucher funds would thus be $3,281,250. Assuming that every voucher user redeems all four vouchers, there would be a maximum of 32,812 participants. Assuming approximately 500,000 registered voters in Seattle, we estimate a voucher participation rate of 6.56 percent.

2. Hajnal, *America's Uneven Democracy*.

3. Berk Consulting, "Seattle Democracy Voucher Program Evaluation."

4. The contribution and overall campaign spending limits are adjusted every two years. In 2020, the SEEC voted to increase the spending limits for at-large and district

City Council seats, and for city attorney candidates. However, the number and value of the democracy vouchers remains unchanged from the program's inception in 2017.

5. This section draws on candidate interviews conducted during the 2023 election cycle.

6. Griffith and Noonen, "Effects of Public Campaign Funding."

7. In this regard, it's important to note the gatekeeping role that the qualification process plays in candidate success. Although most primary candidates pledge to participate in the program, only about 40 percent have qualified to redeem vouchers since 2017. Coupled with the increase in electoral competition noted in the last chapter, this suggests that, regardless of an increase in declared candidates, general election candidates are providing voters with meaningful choices at the ballot box.

8. Sheena S. Iyengar and Mark R. Lepper, "When Choice Is Demotivating: Can One Desire Too Much of a Good Thing?" *Journal of Personality and Social Psychology* 79, no. 6 (December 2000): 995–1006, available at https://doi.org/10.1037/0022-3514.79.6.995.

9. Saul Cunow et al., "Less Is More: The Paradox of Choice in Voting Behavior," *Electoral Studies* 69 (February 2021): 102230, available at https://doi.org/10.1016/j.electstud.2020.102230.

10. Berk Consulting, "2019 Election Cycle Evaluation," 43.

11. Berk Consulting, "2019 Election Cycle Evaluation," 20.

12. Berk Consulting, "2019 Election Cycle Evaluation," 20.

13. Kyle Endres, "Targeted Issue Messages and Voting Behavior," *American Politics Research* 48, no. 2 (March 2020): 317–328, available at https://doi.org/10.1177/1532673X19875694; Eitan D. Hersh, *Hacking the Electorate: How Campaigns Perceive Voters* (Cambridge: Cambridge University Press, 2015); Glenn Kefford et al., "Data-Driven Campaigning and Democratic Disruption: Evidence from Six Advanced Democracies," *Party Politics* 29, no. 3 (May 2023): 448–462, available at https://doi.org/10.1177/13540688221084039.

14. Bob Young, "Seattle Candidate Accused of Defrauding First-in-Nation Democracy-Voucher Program," *Seattle Times*, August 17, 2017, available at https://www.seattletimes.com/seattle-news/times-watchdog/seattle-candidate-accused-of-defrauding-democracy-voucher-program/.

15. Daniel Beekman, "Seattle to Drop Charges in 'Democracy Voucher' Alleged Cheating Case if Former Candidate Adheres to Deal," *Seattle Times*, April 6, 2018, available at https://www.seattletimes.com/seattle-news/politics/if-former-seattle-council-candidate-adheres-to-deal-over-vouchers-charges-would-be-dismissed/.

16. Ari Hoffman, "Seattle's 'Democracy Voucher' Program Harvests Taxpayer Money for Radical Candidates and 'Consultants,'" The Post Millennial, 2021, available at https://thepostmillennial.com/seattles-democracy-voucher-program-harvests-taxpayer-money-for-radical-candidates-and-consultants; Rich Smith, "Here's Who Leads the Mayoral Race in Fundraising," The Stranger, 2021, available at https://www.thestranger.com/slog/2021/05/07/57153730/houston-and-echohawk-lead-in-fundraising-but-they-took-very-different-paths-to-get-there.

17. Paul Queary, "Primary Takeaways: Seattle Mayoral Also-Ran Houston Had More Donors than Voters," Substack newsletter, *The Washington Observer* (blog), August 4, 2021, available at https://washingtonobserver.substack.com/p/primary-takeaways-seattle-mayoral.

18. City of Seattle, "Seattle Open Budget," 2023, available at https://openbudget.seattle.gov/#!/year/2023/operating/0/service.

19. In Seattle, the Democracy Voucher Program's standing staff is overseen by the Seattle Ethics and Elections Commission, the primary rulemaking and regulatory body for matters related to elections and campaign finance. The SEEC is composed of seven citizen volunteers who each serve three-year terms. The commission votes on and formally approves any long-term changes to the Democracy Voucher program with the consent of the program's executive director. In other words, the program's standing staff must regularly communicate program issues to the commission for formal deliberation.

20. Ethics and Elections Commission, City of Seattle, "Candidate and Political Committee Guide: 2021 Election," 2021, available at https://www.seattle.gov/documents/departments/ethicselections/elections/2021candguide.pdf.

21. Gene Balk, "Seattle Tops Major Metros for People Feeling Unsafe in Their Neighborhood," *Seattle Times*, August 2, 2023, available at https://www.seattletimes.com/seattle-news/data/seattle-tops-major-metros-for-people-feeling-unsafe-in-their-neighborhood/; Danny Westneat, "Even Seattle Leaders Don't Know Where to Turn for Homeless Help," *Seattle Times*, August 12, 2023, available at https://www.seattletimes.com/seattle-news/even-seattle-leaders-dont-know-whom-to-call-to-get-homeless-help/.

22. Michael J. Malbin and Thomas Gais, *The Day after Reform: Sobering Campaign Finance Lessons from the American States* (New York: Rockefeller Institute Press, 1998); Miller, *Subsidizing Democracy*.

23. Campaign Legal Center, "*Elster v. City of Seattle*," Campaign Legal Center, June 6, 2018, available at https://campaignlegal.org/cases-actions/elster-v-city-seattle.

24. Harvard Law Review, "*Elster v. City of Seattle*," *Harvard Law Review*, January 10, 2020, available at https://harvardlawreview.org/print/vol-133/elster-v-city-of-seattle/.

25. *Elster and Pynchon v. City of Seattle*, 193 Wn.2d 638.

26. *Buckley v. Valeo*, 442 U.S. (1976).

27. Daniel Beekman, "U.S. Supreme Court Won't Hear Challenge to Seattle's 'Democracy Vouchers,'" *Seattle Times*, March 30, 2020, available at https://www.seattletimes.com/seattle-news/politics/u-s-supreme-court-wont-hear-challenge-to-seattles-democracy-vouchers/.

28. *Citizens United v. Federal Election Commission*, 558 U.S. 310 (2010); *McCutcheon v. Federal Election Commission*, 572 U.S. 185 (2014).

29. James Weinstein, "Campaign Finance Reform and the First Amendment: An Introduction," *Arizona State Law Journal* 34 (2002): 1057.

30. Richard L. Hasen, "*Buckley* Is Dead, Long Live *Buckley*: The New Campaign Finance Incoherence of *McConnell v. Federal Election Commission*," *University of Pennsylvania Law Review* 153, no. 1 (November 2004): 31, available at https://doi.org/10.2307/4150621.

31. "The concept that government may restrict the speech of some elements of our society in order to enhance the relative voice of others is wholly foreign to the First Amendment" (Hasen 2010: 20).

32. *Citizens United v. Federal Election Commission*.

33. Prior to *Citizens United*, Washington state law—and, in turn, local law in Seattle—permitted corporations and labor unions to make contributions and independent expenditures in state and local elections. However, as we demonstrate later, independent expenditure–only committees, or super PACs, became increasingly important in Seattle elections after 2013.

34. Paul S. Herrnson et al., "The Impact of Associational Ties on the Financing of Super PACs," *Interest Groups & Advocacy*, December 7, 2023, available at https://doi.org/10.1057/s41309-023-00199-y.

35. Mike Baker, "Amazon Tests 'Soul of Seattle' with Deluge of Election Cash," *New York Times*, October 30, 2019, available at https://www.nytimes.com/2019/10/30/us /seattle-council-amazon-democracy-vouchers.html.

36. Ethics and Elections Commission City of Seattle, "Democracy Voucher Program: 2023 Candidate Toolkit," 2023, available at https://www.seattle.gov/documents/Depart ments/EthicsElections/DemocracyVoucher/Candidate%20Toolkit/2023%20DVP%20 Candidate%20Toolkit%20FINAL-a_136240.pdf.

37. Jennifer A. Heerwig and Katherine Shaw, "Through a Glass, Darkly: The Rhetoric and Reality of Campaign Finance Disclosure," *Georgetown Law Journal* 102 (2014): 1443–1500.

38. Media accounts of the record-breaking spending highlighted Amazon's opposition to the City Council's proposed Employee Hours Tax (dubbed a "head tax"), which had passed the City Council in 2018 and would have cost high-grossing companies $275 per employee. See Alana Semuels, "How Amazon Helped Kill Seattle a Tax on Business," *The Atlantic*, June 13, 2018, available at https://www.theatlantic.com/technology /archive/2018/06/how-amazon-helped-kill-a-seattle-tax-on-business/562736/.

39. Karen Weise, "The Week in Tech: Amazon Muscles In on Seattle Election," *New York Times*, October 18, 2019, available at https://www.nytimes.com/2019/10/18/tech nology/amazon-seattle-council-election.html.

40. A *foreign-influenced corporation* is defined as: "1. A single foreign owner holds, owns, controls, or otherwise has direct or indirect beneficial ownership of one percent or more of the total equity, outstanding voting shares, membership units, or other applicable ownership interests of the corporation; 2. Two or more foreign owners, in aggregate, hold, own, control, or otherwise have direct or indirect beneficial ownership of five percent or more of the total equity, outstanding voting shares, membership units, or other applicable ownership interests of the corporation; or 3. A foreign owner participates directly or indirectly in the corporation's decision-making process with respect to the corporation's political activities in the United States." City of Seattle, CB 119731, Ord. 126035 (2020), available at https://seattle.legistar.com/Legislation Detail.aspx?ID=4294877&GUID=6920B073-DF76-413B-AA7E-5731BF990F43& FullText=1.

41. Douglas M. Spencer and Abby K. Wood, "Citizens United, States Divided: An Empirical Analysis of Independent Political Spending," *Indiana Law Journal* 89 (2014): 315.

42. Paul S. Herrnson, "The Impact of Organizational Characteristics on Super PAC" (Washington, DC: Bipartisan Policy Center, 2017), available at https://bipartisanpol icy.org/download/?file=/wp-content/uploads/2019/05/The-Impact-of-Organizational -Characteristics-on-Super-PAC-Financing-and-Independent-Expenditures.pdf.

43. For primary campaigns, the program matches small-dollar donations up to $250 with public funds at a rate of 1:1. In the general election, party nominees can receive a lump sum grant up to a set maximum. For instance, the presidential election fund grant would have been $103.7 million in 2020 had any of the candidates chosen to use it. In both cases, participation in the program requires candidates to abide by set spending limits.

44. John C. Green and Nathan S. Bigelow, "The 2000 Presidential Nominations: The Costs of Innovation," in *Financing the 2000 Election*, ed. David B. Magleby (Washington, DC: Brookings Institution Press, 2002).

45. Prior to *Citizens United v. FEC*, outside spending in presidential elections was primarily channeled through 527 and 501(c) organizations.

46. Anthony Corrado, "Financing the 2008 Presidential General Election," in *Financing the 2008 Election: Assessing Reform*, ed. David B. Magleby and Anthony Corrado (Washington, DC: Brookings Institution Press, 2011), available at https://muse.jhu.edu /book/29134.

47. Samuel Issacharoff and Pamela S. Karlan, "The Hydraulics of Campaign Finance Reform," *Texas Law Review* 77, no. 7 (June 1999): 1705.

48. Issacharoff and Karlan, "Hydraulics of Campaign Finance Reform."

49. Federal Election Commission, "Public Funding of Presidential Elections," FEC. gov, 2023, available at https://www.fec.gov/introduction-campaign-finance/under standing-ways-support-federal-candidates/presidential-elections/public-funding-pres idential-elections/.

CONCLUSION

1. Katherine Shaw, "The Lost History of the Millionaire's Amendment," *Election Law Journal: Rules, Politics, and Policy* 16, no. 1 (March 2017): 172–182, available at https:// doi.org/10.1089/elj.2016.0423.

2. Public Ethics Commission, City of Oakland, "Democracy Dollars Program | Oakland Fair Elections Act," City of Oakland, 2023, available at https://www.oaklandca.gov /topics/democracy-dollars.

3. David Moore, "Oakland Community Groups Call to Fund 'Democracy Dollars' Program," *Sludge*, May 25, 2023, available at https://readsludge.com/2023/05/25/oak land-community-groups-call-to-fund-democracy-dollars-program/.

4. City News Service, "LA City Council Seeks a Way to Fund 'Democracy Vouchers' for Voters—Daily News," *Los Angeles Daily News*, June 13, 2023, available at https:// www.dailynews.com/2023/06/13/la-city-council-seeks-a-way-to-fund-democracy -vouchers-for-voters/.

5. San Diego's Voters' Voice Initiative Committee, "Democracy Dollars," Voters' Voice Initiative, 2023, available at https://sdvotersvoice.org/.

6. Unlike the initiative in Seattle, both ballot propositions elicited significant local opposition. In Albuquerque, several conservative organizations—including the Rio Grande Foundation and New Mexico Business Coalition—came out against the proposition. In Austin, local unions and immigrants' rights groups criticized the inclusivity of the democracy dollars proposal.

7. U.S. Census Bureau, "U.S. Census Bureau QuickFacts: Albuquerque City, New Mexico," 2022, available at https://www.census.gov/quickfacts/fact/table/albuquerque citynewmexico/PST045222; Census Bureau, "U.S. Census Bureau QuickFacts: Los Angeles City, California," 2022, available at https://www.census.gov/quickfacts/fact /table/losangelescitycalifornia/PST045222.

8. "HF 3 Status in the House for the 93rd Legislature (2023–2024)," Pub. L. No. HF 3 (2023), available at https://www.revisor.mn.gov/bills/bill.php?f=HF0003&y=2023&ssn= 0&b=house#actions; "HB 263 Virginia Democracy Voucher Program," Pub. L. No. HB 263 (2018), available at https://lis.virginia.gov/cgi-bin/legp604.exe?181+sum+HB263; "New Hampshire House Bill 324," Pub. L. No. HB 324 (2023), available at https://legis can.com/NH/bill/HB324/2023; "HB 1755 - 2023-24," accessed July 18, 2023, available at https://app.leg.wa.gov/billsummary?BillNumber=1755&Initiative=false&Year=2023.

9. Ballotpedia, "South Dakota Revision of State Campaign Finance and Lobbying Laws, Initiated Measure 22 (2016)," Ballotpedia, 2023, available at https://ballotpedia

.org/South_Dakota_Revision_of_State_Campaign_Finance_and_Lobbying_Laws,_In itiated_Measure_22_(2016).

10. U.S. Congress, House, *For the People Act of 2021*, HR 1, 117th Cong., 1st sess. 2021, introduced in House January 4, 2021, available at https://www.congress.gov/bill/117th -congress/house-bill/1/text.

11. U.S. Congress, House, *For the People Act of 2021*, HR 1.

12. U.S. Congress, House, *For the People Act of 2021*, HR 1.

13. Richard L. Hasen, "H.R. 1 Can't Pass the Senate. But Here Are Some Voting Reforms That Could," *Washington Post*, March 16, 2021, available at https://www.wash ingtonpost.com/outlook/2021/03/16/hr-1-voting-reforms/.

14. U.S. Congress, Senate, *An Act to Impose Overall Limitations on Campaign Expenditures and Political Contributions*, S. 3044, 93rd Cong., 2d sess., legislation, October 15, 1974, available at http://www.congress.gov/bill/93rd-congress/senate-bill/3044/all -actions.

15. Nolan McCarty, *Polarization: What Everyone Needs to Know* (Oxford: Oxford University Press, 2019); Nolan McCarty, Keith T. Poole, and Howard Rosenthal, *Polarized America: The Dance of Ideology and Unequal Riches*, 2d ed. (Cambridge, MA: MIT Press, 2016).

Bibliography

Ackerman, Bruce. "Crediting the Voters: A New Beginning for Campaign Finance." *The American Prospect*, April 1, 1993. Available at https://prospect.org/api/content/0b1bf27b -4790-5ff6-9e59-4700ac2aa633/.

Ackerman, Bruce, and Ian Ayres. *Voting with Dollars: A New Paradigm for Campaign Finance*. New Haven, CT: Yale University Press, 2002.

Adamany, David, and George Agree. *Political Money: A Strategy for Campaign Financing in America*. Baltimore: Johns Hopkins University Press, 1975.

Adams, Brian E. *Campaign Finance in Local Elections: Buying the Grassroots*. Boulder, CO: Lynne Rienner Publishers, 2022. Available at https://doi.org/10.1515/9781626371705.

———. "Fundraising Coalitions in Open Seat Mayoral Elections." *Journal of Urban Affairs* 29, no. 5 (December 2007): 481–499. Available at https://doi.org/10.1111/j.1467 -9906.2007.00361.x.

———. "Suburban Money in Central City Elections: The Geographic Distribution of Campaign Contributions." *Urban Affairs Review* 42, no. 2 (November 2006): 267–280. Available at https://doi.org/10.1177/1078087406292699.

Alexander, Herbert E., and Michael C. Walker. *Public Financing of Local Elections: A Data Book on Public Funding in Four Cities and Two Counties*. Los Angeles: Citizens' Research Foundation, University of Southern California, 1990.

Associated Press. "Socialist Sworn In as Seattle City Council Member." *USA Today*, January 6, 2014. Available at https://www.usatoday.com/story/news/nation/2014/01/06 /socialist-seattle-city-council/4349923/.

Atkeson, Lonna Rae, and Nancy Carrillo. "More Is Better: The Influence of Collective Female Descriptive Representation on External Efficacy." *Politics & Gender* 3, no. 1 (March 2007): 79–101. Available at https://doi.org/10.1017/S1743923X0707002X.

Austin, City of. City Clerk. Austin Fair Campaigns, Pub. L. No. 20080925-079, Austin City Code (2008). Available at https://services.austintexas.gov/edims/document .cfm%3Fid%3D121599.

Baker, Andy, and Corey Cook. "Representing Black Interests and Promoting Black Culture: The Importance of African American Descriptive Representation in the U.S. House." *Du Bois Review: Social Science Research on Race* 2, no. 2 (September 2005): 227–246. Available at https://doi.org/10.1017/S1742058X05050162.

Baker, Mike. "Amazon Tests 'Soul of Seattle' with Deluge of Election Cash." *New York Times*, October 30, 2019, U.S. sec. Available at https://www.nytimes.com/2019/10/30/us/seattle-council-amazon-democracy-vouchers.html.

Balk, Gene. "The Seattle Area Has Gotten Even More Liberal—Here's Why." *Seattle Times*, February 24, 2020. Available at https://www.seattletimes.com/seattle-news/data/blue-bump-democratic-supporters-now-make-up-majority-of-adults-in-snohomish-and-king-counties/.

———. "Seattle Tops Major Metros for People Feeling Unsafe in Their Neighborhood." *Seattle Times*, August 2, 2023. Available at https://www.seattletimes.com/seattle-news/data/seattle-tops-major-metros-for-people-feeling-unsafe-in-their-neighborhood/.

———. "Where King County Ranks amid the 'Bluest' Counties in the Nation." *Seattle Times*, November 10, 2022. Available at https://www.seattletimes.com/seattle-news/data/king-county-is-not-the-bluest-big-u-s-county-but-were-close/.

Ballotopedia. "South Dakota Revision of State Campaign Finance and Lobbying Laws, Initiated Measure 22 (2016)." Ballotpedia, 2023. Available at https://ballotpedia.org/South_Dakota_Revision_of_State_Campaign_Finance_and_Lobbying_Laws,_Initiated_Measure_22_(2016).

Bartels, Larry M. *Unequal Democracy: The Political Economy of the New Gilded Age*. 2nd ed. Princeton, NJ: Princeton University Press, 2018.

Beekman, Daniel. "I-122: Big Money Helping Wage Anti-Big-Money Campaign." *Seattle Times*, October 26, 2015, Local Politics sec. Available at https://www.seattletimes.com/seattle-news/politics/i-122-big-money-helping-wage-anti-big-money-campaign/.

———. "Seattle Candidates Again Vie for 'Democracy Vouchers' as They Pivot to November Election." *Seattle Times*, September 6, 2021. Available at https://www.seattletimes.com/seattle-news/politics/seattle-candidates-again-vie-for-democracy-vouchers-as-they-pivot-to-november-election/.

———. "Seattle Initiative Drive Seeks Public Campaign Financing, Reform." *Seattle Times*, April 3, 2015, Local Politics sec. Available at https://www.seattletimes.com/seattle-news/politics/seattle-initiative-drive-seeks-public-campaign-financing-reform/.

———. "Seattle's Richest, Whitest Areas Dominate Campaign Giving, Say Reform Backers." *Seattle Times*, July 21, 2015. Available at https://www.seattletimes.com/seattle-news/politics/seattles-richest-whitest-sway-campaign-giving-say-reform-backers/.

———. "Seattle to Drop Charges in 'Democracy Voucher' Alleged Cheating Case if Former Candidate Adheres to Deal." *Seattle Times*, April 6, 2018. Available at https://www.seattletimes.com/seattle-news/politics/if-former-seattle-council-candidate-adheres-to-deal-over-vouchers-charges-would-be-dismissed/.

———. "U.S. Supreme Court Won't Hear Challenge to Seattle's 'Democracy Vouchers.'" *Seattle Times*, March 30, 2020. Available at https://www.seattletimes.com/seattle-news/politics/u-s-supreme-court-wont-hear-challenge-to-seattles-democracy-vouchers/.

Berk Consulting. "2019 Election Cycle Evaluation." Seattle, WA: Berk Consulting, 2020. Available at https://www.seattle.gov/documents/Departments/EthicsElections/DemocracyVoucher/Biennial%20Reports/Final%20DVP%20Evaluation%20Report%20July23_2020.pdf.

———. "Seattle Democracy Voucher Program Evaluation." Seattle, WA: Berk Consult-

ing, 2018. Available at https://www.seattle.gov/documents/Departments/EthicsElec
tions/DemocracyVoucher/Biennial%20Reports/DVP%20Evaluation%20Final%20
Report%20April%2025%202018.pdf.

Bonica, Adam. "Professional Networks, Early Fundraising, and Electoral Success." *Election Law Journal: Rules, Politics, and Policy* 16, no. 1 (2017): 153–171. Available at https://doi.org/10.1089/elj.2016.0413.

Bowman, Ann. *Reinventing the Austin City Council.* Political Lessons from American Cities. Philadelphia: Temple University Press, 2020.

Bowman, Ann O'M., and Richard C. Kearney. *State and Local Government.* Boston: Cengage Learning, 2016.

Briffault, Richard. "Home Rule and Local Political Innovation." *Journal of Law & Politics* 22 (2006): 1–32.

Buckley v. Valeo, 424 U.S. 1 (1976).

Burgess, Tim. "Public Campaign Finance: Right Idea, Wrong Time." Seattle Forward, 2014. Available at https://www.timburgess.com/2014/06/public-campaign-finance
-right-idea-wrong-time.html.

Cagé, Julia. *The Price of Democracy: How Money Shapes Politics and What to Do about It.* Cambridge, MA: Harvard University Press, 2020.

Campaign Finance Institute. "The Cost of Winning an Election, 1986–2018," 2022. Available at http://www.cfinst.org/pdf/federal/HistoricalTables/pdf/CFI_Federal
-CF_18_Table2-01.pdf.

———. "Table 2-8: House Receipts from Individuals, PACs, and Others, All General Election Candidates, 1999–2018," 2018. Available at http://www.cfinst.org/pdf/fed
eral/HistoricalTables/pdf/CFI_Federal-CF_18_Table2-08.pdf.

Campaign Legal Center. "*Elster v. City of Seattle.*" Washington, DC: Campaign Legal Center, 2018. Available at https://campaignlegal.org/cases-actions/elster-v-city-seattle.

Center for Responsive Politics. "Donor Demographics." OpenSecrets News, 2022. Available at https://www.opensecrets.org/elections-overview/donor-demographics?cycle
=2018&display=A.

———. "Most Expensive Ever: 2020 Election Cost $14.4 Billion." OpenSecrets News, February 11, 2021. Available at https://www.opensecrets.org/news/2021/02/2020
-cycle-cost-14p4-billion-doubling-16/.

Citizens United v. Federal Election Commission, 558 U.S. 310 (2010).

City News Service. "LA City Council Seeks a Way to Fund 'Democracy Vouchers' for Voters—Daily News." *Los Angeles Daily News,* June 13, 2023. Available at https://www.dailynews
.com/2023/06/13/la-city-council-seeks-a-way-to-fund-democracy-vouchers-for-voters/.

Clawson, Dan, Alan Neustadtl, and Mark Weller. *Dollars and Votes: How Business Campaign Contributions Subvert Democracy.* Philadelphia: Temple University Press, 1998.

Colburn, Gregg, and Clayton Page Aldern. *Homelessness Is a Housing Problem: How Structural Factors Explain U.S. Patterns.* Berkeley: University of California Press, 2022.

Connecticut State Elections Enforcement Commission. "Grant Application and Amounts," 2022. Available at https://seec.ct.gov/Portal/CEP/Grants.

Corrado, Anthony. "Financing the 2008 Presidential General Election." In *Financing the 2008 Election: Assessing Reform,* edited by David B. Magleby and Anthony Corrado. Washington, DC: Brookings Institution Press, 2011. Available at https://muse.jhu
.edu/book/29134.

Cunow, Saul, Scott Desposato, Andrew Janusz, and Cameron Sells. "Less Is More: The Paradox of Choice in Voting Behavior." *Electoral Studies* 69 (February 1, 2021): 102230. Available at https://doi.org/10.1016/j.electstud.2020.102230.

Demos. "Public Funding for Electoral Campaigns: How 27 States, Counties and Munici-palities Empower Small Donors and Curb the Power of Big Money in Politics." New York: Demos, 2017. Available at https://www.demos.org/sites/default/files/public ations/Public_Financing_Factsheet_FA%5B5%5D.pdf.

Dupee, Liz, and Alissa Haslam. "The Honest Elections Seattle Story." Unpublished Working Paper, n.d.

Durning, Alan. "Who Funds Seattle's Political Candidates?" Seattle, WA: Sightline Institute, July 2015. Available at https://www.sightline.org/2015/07/22/who-funds -seattles-political-candidates/.

Einstein, Katherine Levine, Maxwell Palmer, and David M. Glick. "Who Participates in Local Government? Evidence from Meeting Minutes." *Perspectives on Politics* 17, no. 1 (March 2019): 28–46. Available at https://doi.org/10.1017/S153759271800213X.

Elster and Pynchon v. City of Seattle, No. 96660-5 (Washington State Supreme Court, 2019).

Endres, Kyle. "Targeted Issue Messages and Voting Behavior." *American Politics Research* 48, no. 2 (March 2020): 317–328. Available at https://doi.org/10.1177/1532673X19875694.

Fleischmann, Arnold, and Lana Stein. "Campaign Contributions in Local Elections." *Political Research Quarterly* 51, no. 3 (September 1998): 673–689. Available at https:// doi.org/10.1177/106591299805100306.

Florida, Richard. *The New Urban Crisis: How Our Cities Are Increasing Inequality, Deep-ening Segregation, and Failing the Middle Class—and What We Can Do About It.* 1st ed. New York: Basic Books, 2017.

Francia, Peter L., John Green, Paul Herrnson, Lynda Powell, and Clyde Wilcox. *The Financiers of Congressional Elections: Investors, Ideologues, and Intimates.* New York: Columbia University Press, 2003.

Francia, Peter L., and Paul S. Herrnson. "The Impact of Public Finance Laws on Fund-raising in State Legislative Elections." *American Politics Research* 31, no. 5 (Septem-ber 2003): 520–539. Available at https://doi.org/10.1177/1532673X03256784.

Gilens, Martin. *Affluence and Influence: Economic Inequality and Political Power in Amer-ica.* Princeton, NJ: Princeton University Press, 2012.

Gilens, Martin, and Benjamin I. Page. "Testing Theories of American Politics: Elites, Interest Groups, and Average Citizens." *Perspectives on Politics* 12, no. 3 (September 2014): 564–581. Available at https://doi.org/10.1017/S1537592714001595.

Goel, Sharad, Marc Meredith, Michael Morse, David Rothschild, and Houshmand Shi-rani-Mehr. "One Person, One Vote: Estimating the Prevalence of Double Voting in U.S. Presidential Elections." *American Political Science Review* 114, no. 2 (May 2020): 456–469. Available at https://doi.org/10.1017/S000305541900087X.

Green, John C., and Nathan S. Bigelow. "The 2000 Presidential Nominations: The Costs of Innovation." In *Financing the 2000 Election*, edited by David B. Magleby. Wash-ington, DC: Brookings Institution Press, 2002.

Greenhouse, Steven. "With Day of Protests, Fast-Food Workers Seek More Pay." *New York Times*, November 30, 2012, New York sec. Available at https://www.nytimes .com/2012/11/30/nyregion/fast-food-workers-in-new-york-city-rally-for-higher-wages .html.

Griffith, Alan, and Thomas Noonen. "The Effects of Public Campaign Funding: Evi-dence from Seattle's Democracy Voucher Program." *Journal of Public Economics* 211 (July 2022): 104676. Available at https://doi.org/10.1016/j.jpubeco.2022.104676.

Grumbach, Jacob M., and Charlotte Hill. "Rock the Registration: Same Day Registration Increases Turnout of Young Voters." *Journal of Politics* 84, no. 1 (January 2022): 405–417. Available at https://doi.org/10.1086/714776.

Grumbach, Jacob M., and Alexander Sahn. "Race and Representation in Campaign Finance." *American Political Science Review* 114, no. 1 (February 2020): 206–221. Available at https://doi.org/10.1017/S0003055419000637.

Haider-Markel, Donald P. "Representation and Backlash: The Positive and Negative Influence of Descriptive Representation." *Legislative Studies Quarterly* 32, no. 1 (2007): 107–133. Available at https://doi.org/10.3162/036298007X202001.

Hajnal, Zoltan L. *America's Uneven Democracy: Race, Turnout, and Representation in City Politics.* Cambridge: Cambridge University Press, 2009.

Hajnal, Zoltan L., and Paul G. Lewis. "Municipal Institutions and Voter Turnout in Local Elections." *Urban Affairs Review* 38, no. 5 (May 2003): 645–668. Available at https://doi.org/10.1177/1078087403038005002.

Hajnal, Zoltan L., and Jessica Trounstine. "Identifying and Understanding Perceived Inequities in Local Politics." *Political Research Quarterly* 67, no. 1 (March 2014): 56–70. Available at https://doi.org/10.1177/1065912913486728.

———. "Where Turnout Matters: The Consequences of Uneven Turnout in City Politics." *Journal of Politics* 67, no. 2 (May 2005): 515–535. Available at https://doi.org/10.1111/j.1468-2508.2005.00327.x.

Harvard Law Review. "*Elster v. City of Seattle.*" *Harvard Law Review*, January 10, 2020. Available at https://harvardlawreview.org/print/vol-133/elster-v-city-of-seattle/.

Hasen, Richard L. "*Buckley* Is Dead, Long Live *Buckley*: The New Campaign Finance Incoherence of *McConnell v. Federal Election Commission.*" *University of Pennsylvania Law Review* 153, no. 1 (November 2004): 31–72. Available at https://doi.org/10.2307/4150621.

———. "H.R. 1 Can't Pass the Senate. But Here Are Some Voting Reforms That Could." *Washington Post*, March 16, 2021. Available at https://www.washingtonpost.com/outlook/2021/03/16/hr-1-voting-reforms/.

Hayes, Matthew, and Matthew V. Hibbing. "The Symbolic Benefits of Descriptive and Substantive Representation." *Political Behavior* 39, no. 1 (March 2017): 31–50. Available at https://doi.org/10.1007/s11109-016-9345-9.

Heerwig, Jennifer A. "Money in the Middle: Contribution Strategies among Affluent Donors to Federal Elections, 1980–2008." *American Journal of Sociology* 123, no. 4 (January 2018): 1004–1063. Available at https://doi.org/10.1086/694888.

Heerwig, Jennifer A., and Brian J. McCabe. "Broadening Donor Participation in Local Elections: Results from the Seattle Democracy Voucher Program in 2021." Washington, DC: McCourt School of Public Policy, Georgetown University, 2022. Available at https://mccourt.georgetown.edu/wp-content/uploads/2022/08/Broadening-Donor-Participation-in-Local-Elections_Report_2022.pdf.

———. "High-Dollar Donors and Donor-Rich Neighborhoods: Representational Distortion in Financing a Municipal Election in Seattle." *Urban Affairs Review* 55, no. 4 (July 2019): 1070–1099. Available at https://doi.org/10.1177/1078087417728378.

Heerwig, Jennifer A., and Katherine Shaw. "Through a Glass, Darkly: The Rhetoric and Reality of Campaign Finance Disclosure." *Georgetown Law Journal* 102, no. 5 (June 2014): 1443. Available at https://dx.doi.org/10.2139/ssrn.2422602.

Herrnson, Paul S. "The Impact of Organizational Characteristics on Super PAC Financing and Independent Expenditures." Paper presented at the Meeting of the Campaign Finance Task Force, Bipartisan Policy Center, Washington, DC, April 21, 2017, rev.

June 2017. Available at https://bipartisanpolicy.org/download/?file=/wp-content/up-loads/2019/05/The-Impact-of-Organizational-Characteristics-on-Super-PAC-Financing-and-Independent-Expenditures.pdf.

Herrnson, Paul S., Jay Goodliffe, Jennifer A. Heerwig, and Douglas M. Spencer. "The Impact of Associational Ties on the Financing of Super PACs." *Interest Groups & Advocacy,* December 7, 2023. Available at https://doi.org/10.1057/s41309-023-00199-y.

Herrnson, Paul S., Costas Panagopoulos, and Kendall L. Bailey. *Congressional Elections: Campaigning at Home and in Washington.* 8th ed. Thousand Oaks, CA: SAGE/CQ Press, 2020.

Hersh, Eitan D. *Hacking the Electorate: How Campaigns Perceive Voters.* Cambridge: Cambridge University Press, 2015.

Hoffman, Ari. "Seattle's 'Democracy Voucher' Program Harvests Taxpayer Money for Radical Candidates and 'Consultants.'" The Post Millennial, September 8, 2021. Available at https://thepostmillennial.com/seattles-democracy-voucher-program-harvests-taxpayer-money-for-radical-candidates-and-consultants.

Holman, Mirya R. "Women in Local Government: What We Know and Where We Go from Here." *State & Local Government Review* 49, no. 4 (2017): 285–296. Available at https://doi.org/10.1177/0160323X17732608.

Honest Elections Seattle. "What Is Initiative 122?" 2015. Available at https://web.archive.org/web/20150427235155/http://honestelectionsseattle.org/what-is-initiative-122/.

Issacharoff, Samuel, and Pamela S. Karlan. "The Hydraulics of Campaign Finance Reform." *Texas Law Review* 77, no. 7 (June 1999): 1705–1738.

Iyengar, Shanto, Tobias Konitzer, and Kent Tedin. "The Home as a Political Fortress: Family Agreement in an Era of Polarization." *Journal of Politics* 80, no. 4 (October 2018): 1326–1338. Available at https://doi.org/10.1086/698929.

Iyengar, Shanto, and Mark R. Lepper. "When Choice Is Demotivating: Can One Desire Too Much of a Good Thing?" *Journal of Personality and Social Psychology* 79, no. 6 (December 2000): 995–1006. Available at https://doi.org/10.1037/0022-3514.79.6.995.

Jacobson, Gary C., and Jamie L. Carson. *The Politics of Congressional Elections.* Lanham, MD: Rowman & Littlefield, 2019.

Jayapal, Pramila. "Committees and Caucuses." *Congresswoman Pramila Jayapal* (blog), 2023. Available at https://jayapal.house.gov/about-me/committees-and-caucuses/.

Joy, Meghan, and Ronald K. Vogel. "Beyond Neoliberalism: A Policy Agenda for a Progressive City." *Urban Affairs Review* 57, no. 5 (September 1, 2021): 1372–1409. Available at https://doi.org/10.1177/1078087420984241.

Kalla, Joshua L., and David E. Broockman. "Campaign Contributions Facilitate Access to Congressional Officials: A Randomized Field Experiment: Field Experiment on Campaign Contributions and Access." *American Journal of Political Science* 60, no. 3 (July 2016): 545–558. Available at https://doi.org/10.1111/ajps.12180.

Kefford, Glenn, Katharine Dommett, Jessica Baldwin-Philippi, Sara Bannerman, Tom Dobber, Simon Kruschinski, Sanne Kruikemeier, and Erica Rzepecki. "Data-Driven Campaigning and Democratic Disruption: Evidence from Six Advanced Democracies." *Party Politics* 29, no. 3 (May 2023): 448–462. Available at https://doi.org/10.1177/13540688221084039.

King County Board of Elections. "Election Results, November 02, 2021," 2021. Available at https://aqua.kingcounty.gov/elections/2021/nov-general/results.pdf.

———. "Election Results, November 03, 2020," 2020. Available at https://aqua.kingcounty.gov/elections/2020/nov-general/results.pdf.

———. "Election Results, November 05, 2019," 2019. Available at https://aqua.kingcoun ty.gov/elections/2019/nov-general/results.pdf.

Kirkland, Patricia A. "Representation in American Cities: Who Runs for Mayor and Who Wins?" *Urban Affairs Review* 58, no. 3 (May 2022): 635–670. Available at https:// doi.org/10.1177/10780874211021688.

Kraus, Jeffrey. "Campaign Finance Reform Reconsidered: New York City's Public Finance Program at Twenty." In *Public Financing in American Elections*, edited by Costas Panagopoulos. Philadelphia: Temple University Press, 2011. Available at http:// www.jstor.org/stable/j.ctt14btbh8.9.

Krebs, Timothy B. "Urban Interests and Campaign Contributions: Evidence from Los Angeles." *Journal of Urban Affairs* 27, no. 2 (June 2005): 165–176. Available at https:// doi.org/10.1111/j.0735-2166.2005.00230.x.

Krebs, Timothy B., and John P. Pelissero. "Fund-Raising Coalitions in Mayoral Campaigns." *Urban Affairs Review* 37, no. 1 (September 2001): 67–84. Available at https:// doi.org/10.1177/10780870122185190.

Laurison, Daniel. "Social Class and Political Engagement in the United States." *Sociology Compass* 10, no. 8 (August 2016): 684–697. Available at https://doi.org/10.1177/0160323 X17732608.

Lessig, Lawrence. "More Money Can Beat Big Money." *New York Times*, November 17, 2011, Opinion sec. Available at https://www.nytimes.com/2011/11/17/opinion/in -campaign-financing-more-money-can-beat-big-money.html.

———. *Republic, Lost: How Money Corrupts Congress—and a Plan to Stop It*. New York: Hachette, 2012.

Malbin, Michael J. "Citizen Funding for Elections: What Do We Know? What Are the Effects? What Are the Options?" Washington, DC: Campaign Finance Institute, 2015. Available at http://www.cfinst.org/pdf/books-reports/CFI_CitizenFunding forElections.pdf.

Malbin, Michael J., Peter W. Brusoe, and Brendan Glavin. "Small Donors, Big Democracy: New York City's Matching Funds as a Model for the Nation and States." *Election Law Journal: Rules, Politics, and Policy* 11, no. 1 (March 2012): 3–20. Available at https://doi.org/10.1089/elj.2010.0099.

Malbin, Michael J., and Thomas Gais. *The Day after Reform: Sobering Campaign Finance Lessons from the American States*. New York: Rockefeller Institute Press, 1998.

Malbin, Michael J., and Michael Parrott. "Small Donor Empowerment Depends on the Details: Comparing Matching Fund Programs in New York and Los Angeles." *The Forum* 15, no. 2 (July 2017): 219–250. Available at https://doi.org/10.1515/for-2017 -0015.

Martin, Casey. "Looking Back at Seattle's CHOP, One Year Later." KUOW, June 7, 2021. Available at https://www.kuow.org/stories/looking-back-at-seattle-s-chop-one-year -later.

McAdam, Doug. *Political Process and the Development of Black Insurgency, 1930–1970*. Chicago: University of Chicago Press, 1999.

McCabe, Brian, and Kenan Dogan. "The Fair Elections Program Is Reshaping the Campaign Finance System in DC, Increasing Candidate and New Donor Participation." McCourt School of Public Policy (blog), September 19, 2021. Available at https:// mccourt.georgetown.edu/news/dc-fair-elections-program/.

McCarty, Nolan. *Polarization: What Everyone Needs to Know*. Oxford: Oxford University Press, 2019.

McCarty, Nolan, Keith T. Poole, and Howard Rosenthal. *Polarized America: The Dance of Ideology and Unequal Riches.* 2nd ed. Cambridge, MA: MIT Press, 2016.

McCutcheon v. Federal Election Commission, 572 U.S. 185 (2014).

McKay, Amy Melissa. "Fundraising for Favors? Linking Lobbyist-Hosted Fundraisers to Legislative Benefits." *Political Research Quarterly* 71, no. 4 (December 2018): 869–880. Available at https://doi.org/10.1177/1065912918771745.

Meyer, David S., and Suzanne Staggenborg. "Movements, Countermovements, and the Structure of Political Opportunity." *American Journal of Sociology* 101, no. 6 (May 1996): 1628–1660. Available at https://doi.org/10.1086/230869.

Miller, Michael G. *Subsidizing Democracy: How Public Funding Changes Elections and How It Can Work in the Future.* Ithaca, NY: Cornell University Press, 2013.

Minnesota Legislature. HF 3. Status in the House for the 93rd Legislature (2023–2024), Pub. L. No. HF 3 (2023). Available at https://www.revisor.mn.gov/bills/bill.php?f=HF0003&y=2023&ssn=0&b=house#actions.

Moore, David. "Oakland Community Groups Call to Fund 'Democracy Dollars' Program." Sludge, May 25, 2023. Available at https://readsludge.com/2023/05/25/oakland-community-groups-call-to-fund-democracy-dollars-program/.

New Hampshire. House. HB324. 2023, Regular Session, Pub. L. No. HB 324 (2023). Available at https://legiscan.com/NH/bill/HB324/2023.

New York City Campaign Finance Board. "Limits & Thresholds | 2021 Citywide Elections," 2021. Available at https://www.nyccfb.info/candidate-services/limits-thresholds/2021/.

Nielsen, Rasmus Klein. "Local Newspapers as Keystone Media: The Increased Importance of Diminished Newspapers for Local Political Information Environments." In *Local Journalism: The Decline of Newspapers and the Rise of Digital Media,* edited by Rasmus Kleis Nielsen. 1st ed. London: I. B. Tauris, 2015.

Oakland, City of. Public Ethics Commission. "Democracy Dollars Program | Oakland Fair Elections Act." City of Oakland, 2023. Available at https://www.oaklandca.gov/topics/democracy-dollars.

Oliver, J. Eric, Shang E. Ha, and Zachary Callen. *Local Elections and the Politics of Small-Scale Democracy.* Princeton, NJ: Princeton University Press, 2012.

O'Neill, Eilis. "Landlords Must Rent First-Come, First-Served." KUOW, November 15, 2019. Available at https://www.kuow.org/stories/landlords-must-rent-first-come-first-served.

OpenSecrets. "Elections Overview, 2020." OpenSecrets News, 2023. Available at https://www.opensecrets.org/elections-overview?cycle=2020&display=T&type=A.

Overton, Spencer. "The Participation Interest." *Georgetown Law Journal* 100 (2012): 1259–1310.

Page, Benjamin I., Larry M. Bartels, and Jason Seawright. "Democracy and the Policy Preferences of Wealthy Americans." *Perspectives on Politics* 11, no. 1 (March 2013): 51–73. Available at https://doi.org/10.1017/S153759271200360X.

Papich, Sarah. "Do Democracy Vouchers Help Democracy?" *Contemporary Economic Policy* 42, no. 1 (2024): 4–24. Available at https://doi.org/10.1111/coep.12625.

Parilla, Joseph, and Glencora Haskins. "Metro Monitor 2023." Brookings, February 2023. Available at https://www.brookings.edu/articles/metro-monitor-2023/.

Portland State University. "Who Votes for Mayor?" 2016. Available at http://whovotesformayor.org/compare.

Powers, Matthew, Sandra Vera Zambrano, and Olivier Baisnée. "The News Crisis Compared: The Impact of the Journalism Crisis on Local News Ecosystems in Toulouse (France) and Seattle (US)." In *Local Journalism: The Decline of Newspapers and the Rise of Digital Media*, edited by Rasmus Kleis Nielsen. 1st ed. London: I. B. Tauris, 2015.

Queary, Paul. "Primary Takeaways: Seattle Mayoral Also-Ran Houston Had More Donors than Voters." Substack newsletter. *The Washington Observer* (blog), August 4, 2021. Available at https://washingtonobserver.substack.com/p/primary-takeaways -seattle-mayoral.

Reingold, Beth, and Jessica Harrell. "The Impact of Descriptive Representation on Women's Political Engagement: Does Party Matter?" *Political Research Quarterly* 63, no. 2 (June 2010): 280–294. Available at https://doi.org/10.1177/1065912908330346.

San Diego Voters' Voice Initiative Committee. "Democracy Dollars." Voters' Voice Initiative, 2023. Available at https://sdvotersvoice.org/.

Schaffner, Brian F., Jesse H. Rhodes, and Raymond J. La Raja. *Hometown Inequality: Race, Class, and Representation in American Local Politics*. Cambridge: Cambridge University Press, 2020.

Schlozman, Kay Lehman, Sidney Verba, and Henry E. Brady. *The Unheavenly Chorus: Unequal Political Voice and the Broken Promise of American Democracy*. Princeton, NJ: Princeton University Press, 2012.

Seattle, City of. CB 119731, Ord 126035 (2020). Available at https://seattle.legistar .com/LegislationDetail.aspx?ID=4294877&GUID=6920B073-DF76-413B-AA7E -5731BF990F43&FullText=1.

———. Charter Amendment 19, City Charter (2013). Available at http://clerk.seattle .gov/~CFs/CF_313380.pdf.

———. "Seattle Open Budget," 2023. Available at https://openbudget.seattle.gov/#!w/year /2023/operating/0/service.

Seattle Ethics and Elections Commission. "Candidate and Political Committee Guide: 2021 Election," 2021. Available at https://www.seattle.gov/documents/departments /ethicselections/elections/2021candguide.pdf.

———. "Democracy Voucher Program: 2023 Candidate Toolkit," 2023. Available at https://www.seattle.gov/documents/Departments/EthicsElections/Democracy Voucher/Candidate%20Toolkit/2023%20DVP%20Candidate%20Toolkit%20FI NAL-a_136240.pdf.

Seattle Municipal Archives. "2015–2019 Ballot Initiatives," 2023. Available at https://www .seattle.gov/cityarchives/seattle-facts/ballot-initiatives#20152019ballotinitiatives.

———. "Ballot Initiatives," 2023. Available at https://www.seattle.gov/cityarchives /seattle-facts/ballot-initiatives.

———. "Brief History of Seattle," 2023. Available at https://www.seattle.gov/cityar chives/seattle-facts/brief-history-of-seattle.

Seattle Office of Labor Standards. "App-Based Worker Paid Sick and Safe Time Ordinance," 2023. Available at https://www.seattle.gov/laborstandards/ordinances/app -based-worker-paid-sick-and-safe-time-ordinance#.

———. "Domestic Workers," 2023. Available at https://www.seattle.gov/laborstandards /ordinances/domestic-workers#:~:text=Seattle%20is%20the%20first%20city,a%20 Domestic%20Workers%20Standards%20Board.

Semuels, Alana. "How Amazon Helped Kill a Seattle Tax on Business." *The Atlantic*, June 13, 2018. Available at https://www.theatlantic.com/technology/archive/2018/06 /how-amazon-helped-kill-a-seattle-tax-on-business/562736/.

Shaw, Katherine. "The Lost History of the Millionaire's Amendment." *Election Law Journal: Rules, Politics, and Policy* 16, no. 1 (March 2017): 172–182. Available at https://doi.org/10.1089/elj.2016.0423.

Skocpol, Theda, and Alexander Hertel-Fernandez. "The Koch Network and Republican Party Extremism." *Perspectives on Politics* 14, no. 3 (September 2016): 681–699. Available at https://doi.org/10.1017/S1537592716001122.

Smith, Rich. "Here's Who Leads the Mayoral Race in Fundraising." The Stranger, 2021. Available at https://www.thestranger.com/slog/2021/05/07/57153730/houston-and-echohawk-lead-in-fundraising-but-they-took-very-different-paths-to-get-there.

———. "Kshama Sawant Says She Won't Use Democracy Vouchers. Why Not?" The Stranger, 2019. Available at https://www.thestranger.com/news/2019/01/24/38277781/kshama-sawant-says-she-wont-use-democracy-vouchers-why-not.

South Lake Union Chamber of Commerce. "Construction & Development." *South Lake Union Chamber of Commerce* (blog), 2023. Available at https://www.sluchamber.org/construction-development/.

Spencer, Douglas M., and Abby K. Wood. "Citizens United, States Divided: An Empirical Analysis of Independent Political Spending." *Indiana Law Journal* 89, no. 1 (Winter 2014): 315–372.

Stone, Clarence N. *Regime Politics: Governing Atlanta, 1946–1988*. Lawrence: University Press of Kansas, 1989.

———. "Urban Regimes and the Capacity to Govern: A Political Economy Approach." *Journal of Urban Affairs* 15, no. 1 (March 1993): 1–28. Available at https://doi.org/10.1111/j.1467-9906.1993.tb00300.x.

Stratmann, Thomas. "Some Talk: Money in Politics. A (Partial) Review of the Literature." *Public Choice* 124, no. 1/2 (July 2005): 135–156. Available at https://doi.org/10.1007/s11127-005-4750-3.

Strauss, David A. "What's the Problem? Ackerman and Ayres on Campaign Finance Reform." *California Law Review* 91, no. 3 (May 2003): 723–741. Available at https://doi.org/10.2307/3481375.

Swindells, Katharine. "Income in US Cities Is Most Unevenly Distributed in a Decade." *City Monitor* (blog), December 22, 2022. Available at https://citymonitor.ai/community/neighbourhoods/us-income-inequality-cities-revealed.

Tate, Katherine. "The Political Representation of Blacks in Congress: Does Race Matter?" *Legislative Studies Quarterly* 26, no. 4 (2001): 623–638. Available at https://doi.org/10.2307/440272.

Ulbig, Stacy G. "Gendering Municipal Government: Female Descriptive Representation and Feelings of Political Trust." *Social Science Quarterly* 88, no. 5 (2007): 1106–1123. Available at https://doi.org/10.1111/j.1540-6237.2007.00494.x.

U.S. Census Bureau. "Congressional Apportionment," 2010 Census Briefs. November 2011. Available at https://www.census.gov/content/dam/Census/library/publications/2011/dec/c2010br-08.pdf.

———. "DP05: ACS Demographic and Housing Estimates," 2021. Available at https://data.census.gov/table?g=160XX00US5363000.

———."DP1: Profile of General Demographic Characteristics: 2000," 2000. Available at https://data.census.gov/table?g=160XX00US5363000&y=2000&tid=DECENNIALDPSF42000.DP1.

———. "S1701: Poverty Status in the Past 12 Months," 2021. Available at https://data.census.gov/table?t=Poverty&g=160XX00US5363000&tid=ACSST1Y2021.S1701.

———. "U.S. Census Bureau QuickFacts: Albuquerque City, New Mexico," 2022. Available at https://www.census.gov/quickfacts/fact/table/albuquerquecitynewmexico /PST045222.

———. "U.S. Census Bureau QuickFacts: Los Angeles City, California," 2022. Available at https://www.census.gov/quickfacts/fact/table/losangelescitycalifornia/PST045222.

———. "U.S. Census Bureau QuickFacts: Seattle City, Washington," 2022. Available at https://www.census.gov/quickfacts/fact/table/seattlecitywashington/PST045222.

U.S. Congress. House. *For the People Act of 2021.* H.R. 1. 117th Cong., 1st sess. Introduced in House January 4, 2021. Available at https://www.congress.gov/bill/117th -congress/house-bill/1/text.

U.S. Congress. Senate. *An Act to Impose Overall Limitations on Campaign Expenditures and Political Contributions Legislation.* S. 3044. 93rd Congress, 2nd sess. October 15, 1974. Available at http://www.congress.gov/bill/93rd-congress/senate-bill/3044 /all-actions.

U.S. Federal Election Commission. "Contribution Limits." FEC.gov, 2022. Available at https://www.fec.gov/help-candidates-and-committees/candidate-taking-receipts /contribution-limits/.

———. "Public Funding of Presidential Elections." FEC.gov, 2023. Available at https:// www.fec.gov/introduction-campaign-finance/understanding-ways-support-federal -candidates/presidential-elections/public-funding-presidential-elections/.

Verba, Sidney, Kay Lehman Schlozman, and Henry E. Brady. *Voice and Equality: Civic Voluntarism in American Politics.* Cambridge, MA: Harvard University Press, 1995.

Virginia General Assembly. 2018 Sess. Pub. L. No. HB 263. Virginia Democracy Voucher Program. Available at https://lis.virginia.gov/cgi-bin/legp604.exe?181+sum+HB263.

Washington State Legislature. "HB 1755 - 2023-24." Accessed July 18, 2023. Available at https://app.leg.wa.gov/billsummary?BillNumber=1755&Initiative=false&Year=2023.

Way, Dan. "Chapel Hill Shuts Down Matching Funds for Local Elections." *Carolina Journal*, September 15, 2011. Available at https://www.carolinajournal.com/chapel -hill-shuts-down-matching-funds-for-local-elections/.

Weinstein, James. "Campaign Finance Reform and the First Amendment: An Introduction." *Arizona State Law Journal* 34 (2002): 1057–1094.

Weise, Karen. "The Week in Tech: Amazon Muscles In on Seattle Election." *New York Times*, October 18, 2019, Technology sec. Available at https://www.nytimes .com/2019/10/18/technology/amazon-seattle-council-election.html.

Westneat, Danny. "Even Seattle Leaders Don't Know Where to Turn for Homeless Help." *Seattle Times*, August 12, 2023. Available at https://www.seattletimes.com/seattle -news/even-seattle-leaders-dont-know-whom-to-call-to-get-homeless-help/.

Young, Bob. "'Democracy Vouchers' Win in Seattle; First in Country." *Seattle Times*, November 3, 2015. Available at https://www.seattletimes.com/seattle-news/politics /democracy-vouchers/.

———. "Seattle Candidate Accused of Defrauding First-in-Nation Democracy-Voucher Program." *Seattle Times*, August 17, 2017. Available at https://www.seattletimes.com /seattle-news/times-watchdog/seattle-candidate-accused-of-defrauding-democracy -voucher-program/.

Index

Jennifer A. Heerwig is Associate Professor of Sociology and Political Science (by courtesy) at Stony Brook University.

Brian J. McCabe is Provost's Distinguished Associate Professor of Sociology at Georgetown University.

www.ingramcontent.com/pod-product-compliance
Lightning Source LLC
Chambersburg PA
CBHW031521270326
41930CB00006B/466